The Thirty Years War

David Arnold	The Age of Discovery 1400–1600
A. L. Beier	The Problem of the Poor in Tudor and Early Stuart England
Martin Blinkhorn	Democracy and Civil War in Spain 1931–39
Martin Blinkhorn	Mussolini and Fascist Italy
Robert M. Bliss	Restoration England 1600–1688
Stephen Constantine	Social Conditions in Britain 1918–1939
Eric J. Evans	Sir Robert Peel
Eric J. Evans	The Great Reform Act of 1832
Eric J. Evans	Political Parties in Britain 1783–1867
John Gooch	The Unification of Italy
Alexander Grant	Henry VII
P. M. Harman	The Scientific Revolution
M. J. Heale	The American Revolution
Ruth Henig	The Origins of the First World War
Ruth Henig	The Origins of the Second World War 1933–1939
Ruth Henig	Versailles and After: Europe 1919–1933
P. D. King	Charlemagne
J. M. MacKenzie	The Partition of Africa 1880–1900
Michael Mullett	Calvin
Michael Mullett	The Counter-Reformation
Michael Mullett	Luther
J. H. Shennan	France Before the Revolution
J. H. Shennan	Louis XIV
David Shotter	Augustus Caesar
John K. Walton	Disraeli
John K. Walton	The Second Reform Act
Michael J. Winstanley	Gladstone and the Liberal Party
Michael J. Winstanley	Ireland and the Land Question 1800–1922
Alan Wood	The Origins of the Russian Revolution
Alan Wood	Stalin and Stalinism
Austin Woolrych	England Without a King 1649–1660

LANCASTER PAMPHLETS

The Thirty Years War

Stephen J. Lee

London and New York

First published 1991 by Routledge
11 New Fetter Lane,
London EC4P 4EE

Simultaneously published in the USA and Canada by Routledge
29 West 35th Street, New York, NY 10001

First published in hardback 2001

Routledge is an imprint of the Taylor & Francis Group

© 1991 Stephen J. Lee
Printed in Great Britain by TJ International Ltd, Padstow, Cornwall

British Library Cataloguing in Publication Data
Lee, Stephen J.
The thirty years war. – (Lancaster pamphlets)
1. Thirty years war. 2. Europe
I. Title II. Series
940.24

Library of Congress Cataloging in Publication Data
Lee, Stephen J.
The Thirty Years War / Stephen Lee.
p.   cm.
Includes bibliographical references and index.
1. Thirty Years' War, 1618–1648. I. Title. II. Title: 30 Years War.
D258.L44 1991
940.2'4--dc20   91–16159

ISBN 0–415–06027–3 (pbk)
ISBN 0–415–26862–1 (hbk)

For Margaret and Charlotte

Contents

Foreword

Lancaster Pamphlets offer concise and up-to-date accounts of major historical topics, primarily for the help of students preparing for Advanced Level examinations, though they should also be of value to those pursuing introductory courses in universities and other institutions of higher education. Without being all-embracing, their aims are to bring some of the central themes or problems confronting students and teachers into sharper focus than the textbook writer can hope to do; to provide the reader with some of the results of recent research which the textbook may not embody; and to stimulate thought about the whole interpretation of the topic under discussion.

Maps and illustrations

1
Outline of the Thirty Years War

This opening chapter provides a brief factual survey of the Thirty Years War. Subsequent chapters give a more detailed explanation of specific events, issues and personalities.

The Bohemian Revolt and the beginning of the War 1618–20

In 1618 the province of Bohemia rose against Austrian rule. The Emperor Matthias, also Archduke of Austria and head of the Austrian branch of the Habsburgs, had incited the revolt by trying to eradicate Protestantism in Bohemia and, at the same time, taking measures to impose full political control by the Emperor from Vienna. Particularly resented was the pressure he had placed on the Bohemian estates to elect Ferdinand of Styria, a leading Catholic, as King of Bohemia.

The rebels immediately established a provisional government and began the search for outside assistance. Ferdinand of Styria was declared deposed and the crown of Bohemia was offered instead to a German sympathiser and co-religionist, the Calvinist Elector Frederick of the Palatinate. Support also came from the Duke of Savoy, who sent 2,000 mercenaries under the leadership of Ernst von Mansfeld, and from Bethlen Tabor, the leader of another revolt against the Habsburgs – in Transylvania. In 1618 Mansfeld captured Pilsen while Bethlen laid siege to Vienna. When, in 1619, Ferdinand

1

of Styria was elected Emperor in succession to Matthias, his position appeared virtually untenable.

During the next two years, however, the situation changed dramatically as Spain came to the assistance of the Emperor. A Spanish army under Spinola invaded the Palatinate in 1620, capturing part of Frederick's German lands and weakening his war effort in Bohemia. Meanwhile, by the Treaty of Munich (1619) Maximilian, Duke of Bavaria, had undertaken to co-ordinate the war effort on behalf of the Emperor by means of the Catholic League which he had formed in 1609. In 1620 several of the Empire's leading Lutheran states, including Saxony, promised in the Treaty of Ulm not to assist Bohemia or the Palatinate. In return, their own security was guaranteed.

Bohemia's fate was now sealed. In 1620 the rebel forces were defeated at White Mountain by the Catholic League, the Emperor and a contingent provided by Saxony. The subjection of Bohemia followed, with the execution of twenty-seven ringleaders, the mass confiscation of rebel lands, and the forcible restoration of Catholicism. Frederick of the Palatinate was deposed and the crown of Bohemia reverted to Ferdinand of Styria, now the Emperor Ferdinand II.

The spread of the War to Germany 1619–23

The link between Bohemia and the German part of the Empire was the Elector Frederick of the Palatinate. As soon as he accepted the crown of Bohemia he exposed his German lands to the combined wrath of the Catholic League, Austria and Spain. This was, in fact, the outcome of over half a century of religious confrontation between Catholicism and Calvinism. The Palatinate had been the centre from which Calvinism had spread through the Rhineland and it had been the leading member of the Evangelical Union, a defensive alliance established in 1608. The Emperor and Maximilian's Catholic League now took the opportunity to eradicate what they saw as a major political and ideological threat. Frederick's resources were utterly inadequate to meet the onslaught. The Lutheran states refused to assist and the mercenary forces of Mansfeld, already defeated in Bohemia, were, for the time being, withdrawn from the conflict. The support for the Palatinate came from Baden and Brunswick, but these were quickly overcome by the Bavarian commander, Tilly. Baden pulled out after the Battle of Wimpfen (1622) and Brunswick after Höchst (1622) and Stadlöhn (1623).

Nothing now stood in the way of the conquest of the Palatinate. Spanish and Bavarian troops captured its capital, Heidelberg, in 1622 and Frederick sought sanctuary in the Dutch Republic. Maximilian of Bavaria received Frederick's territories and, for the duration of his lifetime, the coveted title of Elector. It seemed that, five years after its outbreak, the conflict had been resolved in favour of the Emperor and the Catholic League.

The Danish War 1624–9

The very success of the Catholic League, however, helped precipitate the next stage of the War. Tilly's conquests in northern and central Germany posed a serious threat to the Lutheran states in the Baltic. Christian IV of Denmark, in particular, saw himself as the protector of the Lower Saxon Circle, with which he now hastened to form a military alliance. In 1625 he also gained, by the Treaty of the Hague, the support of England and France, which were becoming increasingly concerned about the Habsburg threat, and the Dutch Republic, which was again involved, after a brief interlude, in a struggle for independence from Spain.

Meanwhile, the Emperor Ferdinand II had discovered in Albrecht von Wallenstein a new military commander, who was prepared both to dedicate himself to the Imperial cause and to raise 50,000 men from his own resources. The conflict was now between Denmark, Brunswick, Mansfeld's mercenaries and Bethlen Tabor on the one hand and, on the other, the Catholic League, led by Tilly, the Imperial troops under Wallenstein, and Spain.

Again the issue was decided quickly. In 1626 Wallenstein defeated Mansfeld at Dessau Bridge and Tilly defeated the Danes at Lutter. The Habsburgs appeared unassailable as Tilly proceeded to overrun Denmark, and Wallenstein reached the north German coastline, seizing Wismar and Rostock although failing in his effort to take Stralsund. Confronted by the prospect of total catastrophe if he struggled on, Christian IV withdrew Denmark from the War. By the Peace of Lübeck (1629) he gave up all claim to north German territory, including all ecclesiastical estates. In return, he was permitted to keep his hereditary lands of Schleswig

3

Map 1 Main phases of the War

(a) 1618–23

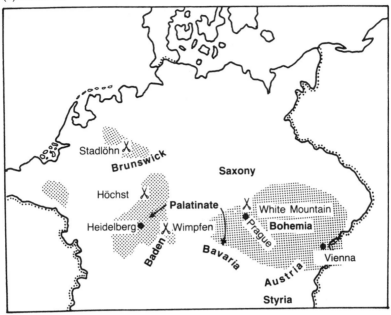

⌁⌁⌁ Boundary of Holy Roman Empire   ⣿ Main areas of fighting

(b) 1625–9

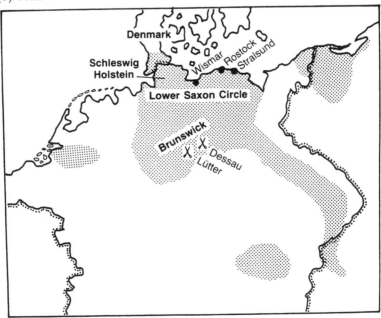

4

(c) 1630–4

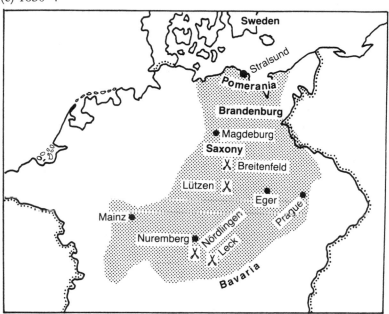

(d) 1635–48

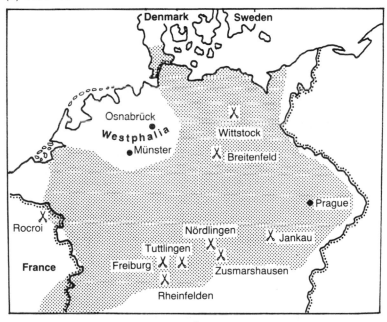

5

and Holstein and was spared the indignity of having to pay reparations.

During the brief lull in hostilities Ferdinand II imposed the Edict of Restitution (1629) which sought to restore to Catholic authority all Church lands which had been secularised since 1552. This stirred up both fear and resentment in northern Germany, a danger foreseen by Wallenstein, who had warned against pinning settlements on ideology. Within a year it had become clear that there was a basis for future revolt against Imperial authority. At the same time, the Emperor came under severe diplomatic pressure at the Diet of Ratisbon, or Regensburg (1630), at which the French delegate, Father Joseph, succeeded in sowing among the German princes discontent with Imperial power.

The Emperor was thus once again vulnerable. To make matters worse, he was persuaded to dismiss the Imperial commander-in-chief. Pressure had been brought to bear against Wallenstein from three quarters: the Jesuits at Ferdinand's court; the Catholic League, which suspected his loyalty to their cause; and Maximilian of Bavaria. Wallenstein went home to his estates in Bohemia convinced, nevertheless, that his recall would be only a matter of time.

The Swedish War 1630–5

The defeat of Denmark and the arrival of Habsburg power on the Baltic coastline were watched with alarm by Gustavus Adolphus, who committed Sweden to the War in 1630. His invasion of northern Germany was accompanied by alliances with the Pro-testant states of Pomerania, Hesse-Cassel and Stralsund. Then, in 1631, he drew up the Treaty of Bärwalde with France which, although Catholic, was profoundly suspicious of Habsburg ac-tivities in central Europe. In return for French subsidies, he undertook to maintain an army in Germany, to concentrate his attention on the Emperor and to refrain from attacking Bavaria.

Two German states, Saxony and Brandenburg, remained neutral throughout 1630 but hastened to join Sweden after Tilly's troops captured, sacked and destroyed the city of Magdeburg. The year 1631 saw the first great victory of the Protestant cause as the combined armies of Saxony and Sweden defeated Tilly at Breitenfeld near Leipzig. The Empire was now wide open to further Swedish advance and the Emperor, conscious at last of his vulnerability, swallowed his pride and reinstated Wallenstein.

Gustavus Adolphus then proceeded to invade the Rhineland and to capture Mainz. Next, in violation of the Treaty of Bärwalde, he crossed into Bavaria. Tilly tried to prevent this but was defeated in 1632 at Leck, where he died of his wounds. Wallenstein, however, slowed down the Swedes' offensive by inflicting a limited defeat on them at Nuremberg. Gustavus Adolphus had to end his campaigns in southern Germany and to march northwards to prevent Elector John George of Saxony from being detached from the War by the Imperialists. At the end of 1632 the Swedes won a hard fought victory at Lützen but suffered, in the process, a grievous blow, for Gustavus Adolphus was killed in the battle. Wallenstein escaped with his life but was dismissed a second time in 1634 and was assassinated in the same year at Eger.

The death of Gustavus Adolphus weakened the Swedish war effort. Although the Swedish Chancellor, Oxenstierna, organised a number of Protestant German states into the League of Heilbronn in 1633, this was smashed at Nördlingen in 1634 when a combination of Spanish, Imperialist and Bavarian troops defeated the Swedes and their German allies. One after another the German states dropped out of the war. Saxony made a separate peace with the Emperor at Prague in 1635, while the Swedish offensive had ground temporarily to a halt.

The Franco-Swedish Phase 1635–48

This was the moment when the French first minister, Cardinal Richelieu, decided to intervene. His main fear was that Sweden's exhaustion would lead to her withdrawal and to a Habsburg revival. After the disaster of Nördlingen he therefore hastened to renew with Oxenstierna the Treaty of Bärwalde, and planned a major attack on the Empire, based on alliances with the Dutch Republic, Bernard of Saxe-Weimar, and the north Italian states of Mantua, Savoy, Parma and Modena.

The French, however, suffered initial reverses. Their invasion of the Rhineland was repulsed by Spanish and Imperialist troops, who entered France and in 1636 threatened Paris. Within a year, however, France had recovered sufficiently to eject the invaders and resume the offensive. Between 1637 and 1648 the Spanish and Austrian branches of the Habsburgs both suffered a series of major defeats in what was to become the most destructive phase of the entire war.

Spain was particularly badly affected. In 1639 a Spanish fleet was destroyed at the Downs by the English and Dutch, while 1643 saw one of the decisive battles of modern history, when the French confirmed at Rocroi their own military ascendancy and Spanish decline. The overall effect of the Franco-Spanish struggle was to detach Spain from the Imperial and Catholic cause and to expose the Emperor to the full onslaught of the Franco-Swedish alliance.

The Empire experienced the most wretched decade in its entire history as it was subjected to repeated and destructive invasion. The Imperial troops were defeated in 1636 by the Swedes at Wittstock and again in 1638 at Rheinfelden; they were then confronted by another French invasion of the Rhineland. In 1642 the Swedes invaded Bohemia and in the same year they defeated the Emperor at the second Battle of Breitenfeld. For a while Bavaria managed to reverse the trend with victories against the French at Tuttlingen (1643), Freiburg (1644) and Mergentheim (1645). However, in 1645 Franco-Swedish forces defeated Bavaria and the Emperor at the second Battle of Nördlingen, and the Swedes won a further victory at Jankau. In desperation Maximilian withdrew Bavaria from the War by the Truce of Ulm (1647). When he changed his mind the following year and re-entered the conflict, Bavarian and Imperial forces were comprehensively defeated at Zusmarshausen. Faced with the capture of Prague by the Swedes, the Emperor was forced in 1648 to agree to the terms of the Treaties of Münster and Osnabrück, known collectively as the Peace of Westphalia. This did not, however, end the war between France and Spain, which continued until the Treaty of the Pyrenees in 1659.

2
Motives of the participants

There are three components to the analysis in this chapter. The Thirty Years War was sparked by revolts against Habsburg rule in the west and east of the Holy Roman Empire. The conflict then spread into the German core of the Empire, where half a century of constitutional and religious dispute had gradually produced two distinct groupings. Meanwhile, the major powers were being drawn one by one into the struggle against the Habsburgs for a combination of dynastic, strategic and religious reasons.

Rebellions in the Netherlands and Bohemia

The catalyst for war is often rebellion, since internal conflict can easily spread across frontiers to involve other states. The powers on the defensive in the Thirty Years War were Spain and Austria, who stood to gain nothing from the destabilisation of central Europe. It was very much in their interest to maintain the status quo which had ensured their ascendancy and to overcome two serious challenges. One, in the east of the Empire, was the Bohemian uprising against Austrian rule; the other, in the west, was the more prolonged Dutch revolt against Spain.

The Bohemian uprising of 1618 was the culmination of a long period of political and religious instability. This went as far back as 1526, when Bohemia had been added to the possessions of the Habsburgs in central Europe. The province contained a wide variety of religious groupings. In addition to the Catholic population, who comprised about 10 per cent of the total, there were four types of Protestant: the Utraquists, the Bohemian Brethren, and the more mainstream Calvinists and Lutherans. The Emperors Ferdinand I and Maximilian II had wisely avoided religious confrontation by allowing a degree of toleration and choosing to concentrate, instead, on consolidating Habsburg political control. The result had been a balance which was, nevertheless, delicate and, in the wrong hands, likely to suffer sudden upset.

During the opening two decades of the seventeenth century Habsburg policies became less cautious and increasingly inconsistent. This was due partly to the bitter rivalry between Emperor Rudolf II and his brother Matthias. In 1609 Rudolf sought the support of the Bohemian Estates against Matthias by guaranteeing, in the Letter of Majesty, freedom of worship. This was, however, a tactical move and by 1611 Rudolf felt strong enough to revoke his promise. The Estates promptly turned to Matthias, whom they elected King of Bohemia in return for a similar undertaking on his part. When he became Emperor in 1612 it appeared that Matthias would soon return Bohemia to the pragmatic policies of the late sixteenth century.

The situation, however, deteriorated rapidly. Matthias, who was childless, sought to make a relative, Ferdinand of Styria, heir apparent to the Imperial throne. The first stage was to force the reluctant Estates to elect Ferdinand King of Bohemia. Once instated, Ferdinand immediately introduced policies to enforce full Austrian control and to undermine Protestantism. Censorship was imposed, non-Catholics were excluded from public office, and several Protestant foundations were declared illegal. The last straw was Ferdinand's refusal to consider a petition from a Protestant assembly seeking to reverse this ban. This provoked a deliberate act of defiance against Austrian rule; in an incident known as the Defenestration of Prague the Imperial Regents were thrown out of a high window in one of the turrets of the Hradschin Palace in Prague.

The Dutch Revolt had broken out during the 1560s as a protest against attempts by Philip II to raise extra taxation, to enforce Catholicism by means of the Inquisition, and to maintain a Spanish army of occupation. By the time of his death in 1598 this policy had clearly failed and his successor, Philip III, was confronted by an Eighty Years War which overlapped the wider, but shorter, European conflict. Although a truce was negotiated in 1611, the conflict was resumed ten years later, shortly after the defeat of the Czechs at the Battle of White Mountain in 1620.

The reactivated struggle exerted a major influence on the course of the Thirty Years War. In the first place, the Dutch Republic was the centre of several major coalitions against the Habsburgs. In 1625, for example, it was a founding member of the Hague Coalition, which comprised France, Denmark and England; in 1631 it formed a treaty with Sweden; and in 1635 it entered an alliance with France. Second, the earlier military innovations of Maurice of Orange considerably influenced the tactics used by the forces of the Protestant states in the War, while the Dutch themselves won a number of naval victories against Spain, effectively threatening the latter's sea routes to Flanders and imperilling the political position of Philip III's first minister, Olivares.

It would be hard to ascribe to Bohemia the same continuing influence as that exerted by the Dutch Republic. After the rebels' initial successes, the Habsburg reconquest of Bohemia was completed. Far from being an equivalent to the Dutch ulcer which sapped Spanish energy, Bohemia was, for much of the War, a storehouse used by Imperial commanders like Wallenstein to replenish the Habsburg war effort. It was for this reason that the province was the target of several Swedish invasions, although it never fell for any length of time under foreign occupation.

The spread to the German states

The Bohemian Revolt was, for two reasons, the catalyst for the spread of the War within the Empire.

In the first place, the Provisional Government, which was established after the Defenestration of Prague, drew in the Palatinate

11

by offering the Bohemian crown to the Elector Frederick. Traditionally the most prestigious of the German states, with one of the six Imperial electoral votes, the Palatinate straddled the area between the Austrian frontier and the Rhineland. When he committed his German possessions to Bohemia, Frederick threw down a double challenge. In siding with the rebels he was in effect declaring war on the Austrian Habsburgs who claimed Bohemia as part of their patrimony. And, by accepting the crown, he was also defying the authority of the Holy Roman Emperor, to whom he owed political allegiance. The Austrian Habsburgs could hardly have been expected to countenance either the loss of one of their own possessions or the probable collapse of Imperial rule. The question was not therefore whether, but when and how, they would retaliate.

This is a traditional and widely held view. A second argument, advanced more recently by P. Brightwell, is that the key factor in the spread of the war to Germany was the military involvement of Spain. The Austrian Habsburgs were in no position to attack the Palatinate, as their early reverses at the hands of the rebels indicated. They were therefore heavily dependent on assistance provided by Philip III, who was influenced by the arguments in favour of intervention advanced by one of his leading councillors, Balthasar de Zuñiga. There was, of course, an obvious dynastic and religious connection between the Austrian and Spanish Habsburgs, but what was also needed was the extra incentive of Spanish self-interest. Of particular importance to Spain was the possible impact of the Bohemian Revolt on the Dutch Republic. If the uprising succeeded, the whole of Germany would be destabilised, the Spanish military routes through the Rhineland would be cut, and there would be no chance of reimposing Spanish rule over the Dutch; it was even possible that the southern Netherlands might also be lost. If, on the other hand, Bohemia and the Palatinate could be subdued, Spain's position in Germany and the Low Countries would be immeasurably strengthened. In 1620, therefore, Spanish troops were ordered into the Palatinate.

The result was a German war which gradually brought in other combatants. The Palatinate was backed by Baden and Brunswick, while the Emperor and Spain were assisted by Germany's leading Catholic state, Bavaria. The Elector of Saxony helped put down the Bohemian uprising but, with Brandenburg, remained aloof from the German conflict until 1631. For the next four years these north German states made common cause with Sweden, before withdrawing again in 1635. Between 1636 and 1648 they alternated between supporting the Emperor and Sweden.

The reasons for this internecine struggle have so far been confined to immediate factors. But, in addition to explaining *how* the Bohemian Revolt spread into the rest of the Empire, it is also necessary to focus on *why* the potential for such a link existed at all. This involves an analysis of the long-term factors which contributed to the Empire's state of political anarchy.

In the first place, the constitutional structure of the Holy Roman Empire had fallen into serious disrepair during the preceding century. The authority of the Emperor had been under continuous challenge from individual state rulers, particularly those who had used the Reformation as an opportunity to assert their autonomy. The institutions of the Empire had, for the time being, folded up under the combined impetus of decentralisation and inter-state rivalries. The first to go was the executive, or *Reichsregiment*, which ceased to function altogether in 1530. The central judiciary, or *Reichskammergericht*, was temporarily put out of action when in 1598 the Emperor refused to consult it over his decision to remove the Protestant mayor and councillors of Aachen. Applying the Emperor's power in this way succeeded only in hastening the end of the Empire as any sort of constitutional unit. The third, and most important organ was the *Reichstag*, or Imperial Diet, which had for centuries acted as the legislature. This suspended itself in 1608 after a major row involving the transfer of the city of Donauwörth to Bavarian supervision.

The collapse of the Empire's already loose constitutional structure was accelerated by the polarisation of individual states into rival confessional units. Although the conflict between Lutherans and Emperor had been ended in 1555 by the Peace of Augsburg, a second phase of rivalry developed in the second half of the sixteenth century, this time between Calvinism and Catholicism. Centred on the Palatinate, Calvinism proved more militant and expansionist than Lutheranism, spreading rapidly to Nassau, Hesse and Anhalt; it was a source of inspiration in the Dutch revolt against Spain from 1568 onwards.

At the other extreme to radical Protestantism stood the equally assertive Catholicism of the Counter Reformation, the German centre of which was Bavaria. The Dukes of Bavaria acted as the instruments of the Emperor against any perceived violation of the Peace of Augsburg and assumed the role of Imperial bulwark against Protestantism, whether in its Calvinist or its Lutheran form. The result was the gradual emergence of two sides which were given military form in opposing confessional alliances. The Evangelical Union was set up in 1608 by the Calvinist states, while the Catholic League, comprising Bavaria, the ecclesiastical states and Würzburg, followed in 1609.

The involvement of the great powers against the Habsburgs

The efforts of Austria and Spain to maintain the status quo attracted the unwelcome attention of three powers on the periphery of the Empire: Denmark, Sweden and France.

Denmark

Denmark had traditionally been the most important of the Baltic states, although her hegemony was, in the opening years of the seventeenth century, in the process of passing to her neighbour, Sweden. Denmark's intervention in the Thirty Years War was in reality her last attempt to pursue a role in Germany. The prospect of territorial aggrandisement was undoubtedly attractive. As Duke of Holstein as well as King of Denmark, Christian IV was already an influential member of the North Saxon Circle. He was unable, however, to resist the prospect of snatching, from the confusion of the mid-1620s, Halberstadt, Verden, Minden, Bremen, Lübeck and Hamburg. These would have enabled Denmark to dominate the outlets of the Rivers Elbe and Weser and thereby the commerce of northern Germany. In the process she would be rescuing German Lutherans from the reconversion to Catholicism which would follow any permanent Habsburg victory. There was also a personal factor. Christian aspired to be the leading statesman of Europe; he was in a position to indulge this particular ambition since frugal management had ensured a healthy financial balance. Finally, he acted with some urgency since he was certain that Gustavus Adolphus was on the point of involving Sweden in the war. This would, of course, reduce the rewards which Christian was certain Denmark could gain.

Subsequent events demonstrated all too clearly the rashness of

Christian's decision. Denmark was heavily defeated by Tilly at Lutter (1626) and was then invaded by the forces of the Catholic League. Forced out of the war by the Treaty of Lübeck (1629), Denmark was obliged to abandon forever any hope of becoming a German power. Instead, she had to defend her position in the Baltic against Sweden in a conflict between the two Lutheran states which lasted from 1643 to 1645. By this stage Sweden had been involved in the Thirty Years War for over a decade. Her contribution was far more substantial than Denmark's, and signalled the rise of a formidable military power in the north.

Sweden

At first, Sweden had been reluctant to intervene; despite the sympathy he felt for Elector Frederick of the Palatinate, Gustavus Adolphus had been compelled to concentrate on Poland, which was considered far more of a threat than Austria during the 1620s. This changed with the defeat of Denmark and the triumphs of the armies of Tilly and Wallenstein in northern Germany. Gustavus Adolphus made peace with Poland in 1629 and switched his resources to a large-scale invasion of the Empire in 1630, making sure by the Treaty of Bärwalde (1631) of a continuous flow of subsidies from France.

Sweden's primary concern was strategic. Gustavus Adolphus said in 1629:

> 'Denmark is used up. The Papists are on the Baltic; they have Rostock, Wismar, Stettin, Wolgast, Griefswald, and nearly all the other ports in their hands; Rügen is theirs, and from Rügen they continue to threaten Stralsund; their whole aim is to destroy Swedish commerce, and plant a foot on the southern shore of our Fatherland. Sweden is in danger from the power of the Habsburg.'

An additional, but closely related, motive was to save German Lutheranism; 'as one wave follows another, so the Catholic League batters at our gates.' There has been some controversy as to whether Gustavus Adolphus was driven by religious zeal or whether his aims were purely political. This is, however, an artificial distinction. Religious concern was normally in harmony with political considerations since Lutheranism was an essential

15

component of the Swedish state, the state in turn being seen as the protector of the official religion.

A third reason for Swedish involvement in the War was the possibility of succeeding, where Denmark had failed, in dominating Germany. It has to be said, however, that this was not an immediate priority; rather, it became a distinct possibility once the Swedes had established themselves in Pomerania. At first, Gustavus Adolphus thought in terms of gaining the permanent support of the Lutheran states. In 1630, therefore, he drew up a list of fourteen points guaranteeing the integrity of the individual units within the Empire. Clearly, he hoped at this stage to establish his reputation as a protector and mediator. When this brief attempt at diplomacy failed, he turned to military alliances with Pomerania, Mecklenburg, Hesse-Cassel and Stralsund, followed in 1631 by agreements with Saxony and Brandenburg. After his spectacular military success at Breitenfeld in 1631, he began to think in terms of establishing a new Germany under Swedish influence. His *Norma Futurarum Actionum* contained proposals to destroy the Habsburg grip on Germany and to set up a new Protestant union to defy the power of Catholicism. A Swedish-controlled confederation would be established, consisting both of Protestant states and of Catholic states to be conquered in the future. The death of Gustavus Adolphus at Lützen in 1632 interrupted this design, although Oxenstierna sought in the League of Heilbronn to create an alliance of Protestant states. The League was, however, shattered by the great Habsburg victory at Nördlingen in 1634. Many German states followed the example set by Saxony in 1635 in making peace with the Emperor. Sweden was thus deprived of any pretext to act as the protector of German interests.

During the last phase of the War Swedish aims became increasingly territorial, as Swedish diplomats at Westphalia placed a high price on making peace with the beleaguered Emperor. The success of Sweden's armies in the 1640s, together with the self-interest shown by former allies like Brandenburg and Saxony, meant that Sweden became as openly pragmatic as France.

France

The involvement of France in the Thirty Years War was related directly to her struggles with the Habsburgs during the sixteenth century. The latter had acquired substantial territories scattered across central and western Europe, some of them directly adjacent to France. Before 1559 there had been intermittent but intensive warfare until the temporary compromise of the Treaty of Câteau-Cambrésis. This, however, proved to be no more than an armistice. The Wars of Religion had preoccupied France for the rest of the sixteenth century, but during the reigns of Henry IV (1589–1610) and Louis XIII (1610–43) French foreign policy once again focused on the Habsburgs.

The threat was analysed by Cardinal Richelieu, First Minister to Louis XIII. The Habsburgs and their dependencies flanked France in two arcs (see Map 2). The inner arc, directly against the French frontier, comprised Spain, Franche Comté and the Spanish Netherlands. The outer arc included Naples, Milan, Austria, Styria, Tyrol and Bohemia, together with several states – like Tuscany and Genoa – which were ruled by relatives of the Habsburgs. As a result, the Habsburgs controlled several strategic positions from which attacks could be launched against France. Richelieu set three main objectives for French policy. The first was to deal with the immediate Habsburg threat. 'It is necessary', he said, 'to have a perpetual design to arrest the progress of Spain'; he intended also 'to halt the advance of the House of Austria'. At the same time, he wanted to gain allies in Europe and to extend the influence of France by diplomacy where possible and by war where necessary. His third objective was in the longer term to build territorial bridgeheads to enable future French expansion into the Holy Roman Empire; he had a particular interest in Alsace, Lorraine, Franche Comté, Artois and Flanders.

Although fully conscious of the Habsburg threat, Richelieu did not commit France to the War during the 1620s and early 1630s. The main reason was his preoccupation during this period with a series of domestic priorities – the revival of royal power, the restoration of financial solvency, and the elimination of the threat from the Huguenots. He therefore concentrated on weakening the position of the Habsburgs by diplomacy and peripheral military involvement. One method was to subsidise the struggle of other powers against Spain and Austria. For example, the Treaty of Compiègne (1624) provided assistance to enable the Dutch to renew their war with Spain, while the Treaty of Bärwalde (1631) financed Sweden's war effort in Germany for six years. Richelieu also resorted

17

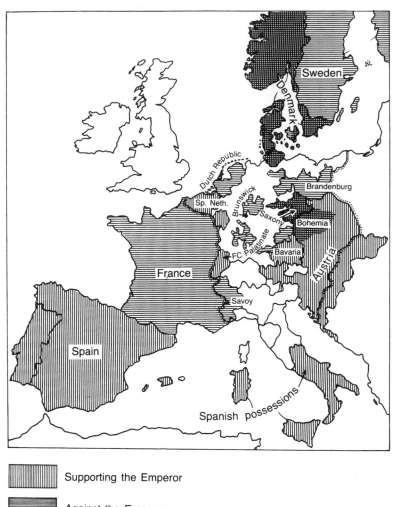

Sweden

Denmark

Dutch Republic

Brandenburg

Sp. Neth.

Brunswick

B

Saxony

Bohemia

FC Palatinate

Bavaria

France

Austria

Savoy

Spain

Spanish possessions

Supporting the Emperor

Against the Emperor

Changed sides during the War

Boundary of Holy Roman Empire

Map 2 Protagonists in the War

18

to diplomatic intrigues through conference diplomacy. Through his delegate, Father Joseph, Richelieu scored several successes for France at the Diet of Ratisbon in 1630. He managed temporarily to detach Bavaria from the Imperial alliance, to undermine the credibility of Wallenstein as Imperial commander, and to cause severe embarrassment to the Emperor by persuading the German Electors to refuse to confer on Ferdinand's son the title of King of the Romans.

By 1635 it had become clear that French intervention was necessary to prevent a major Habsburg revival. The coalition between Sweden and the German states had been smashed at Nördlingen in 1634, and the Peace of Prague the following year between the Emperor and Saxony threatened the end of all hostilities. It was far from certain that Oxenstierna would want to commit Sweden to a war which was becoming increasingly expensive – unless, of course, a new alliance could be formed against the Habsburgs. Richelieu therefore had to switch from diplomacy and subsidies to a more direct military option. There was an additional motive for intervening at this stage. Sweden and the Habsburgs had exhausted each other and there was every prospect for France of swift military success and territorial gain. Richelieu also expected France to be by far the strongest partner in the new anti-Habsburg coalition, which included Sweden, the Dutch Republic, Bernard of Saxe-Weimar and the north Italian states of Savoy, Mantua, Modena and Parma. France would therefore be able to dictate terms and, in the process, prevent Sweden from replacing the Habsburgs as a major political force in the Empire. Subsequent events showed that France's initial priority had in fact to be a struggle for survival against the Spanish invasion of 1636. Her recovery was swift, culminating in a victory over the Spanish army at Rocroi in 1643. Even so, French gains at Westphalia were probably fewer than Richelieu had anticipated and it was not until the Treaty of the Pyrenees (1659) that his policies appeared to have been fully vindicated.

What was the main cause of the War?

So far this chapter has analysed the various rivalries and explained how they interacted to produce a conflict involving smaller states and European powers. When it comes to trying to identify from these components what was the main cause of the Thirty Years War, there is, inevitably, some controversy.

The main conflict of opinion has been between historians who adopt a German focus and those who prefer one which is more distinctively European. The traditional view is that the main influences exerted came from the Empire, with the external powers being pulled into the conflict by developing circumstances. C. V. Wedgwood, for example, maintained that 'Germany's tragedy was essentially her own. Without extenuating the actions of Richelieu, Olivarez, the two Ferdinands and the King of Sweden, it is yet possible to see that the opportunity was made for them and not by them.' This approach has, however, invited criticism from three directions.

First, there have been attempts to shift the focus within, rather than outside, the Empire. J. V. Polisensky, for example, sought to redress what he regarded as an excessively German approach by concentrating on the origins and initial phase of the conflict. This strengthened the focus on Bohemia, the problems and aspirations of which were an essential prerequisite for both the German and the European conflicts.

Second, and more recently, the War has been seen as a struggle between the European powers which happened to take place within the confines of the Empire. According to G. Pagès, the prime mover in this was France, involved, indirectly from 1629 and directly from 1635, in a conflict for supremacy against the Habsburgs. An even more ardent exponent of this view has been S. H. Steinberg, who argued:

> The Thirty Years War was never exclusively, or even primarily, a German affair but concerned the whole of Europe. It was to some extent, a by-product of France's efforts, after the conclusion of her religious war, to break her encirclement by the Habsburg powers of Spain and Austria. What happened was that some regions of Germany, but never the whole Empire, intermittently took a direct part in, or were drawn into, the various hot and cold wars and the diplomatic and ideological conflicts between the houses of Bourbon and Austria.

P. Brightwell and J. Elliott have followed a similar approach, although they have attached more significance than Pagès and Steinberg to the intervention of Spain and to the influence of de

Zuñiga and Olivares as well as that of Richelieu and Mazarin.

In 1988 M. P. Gutmann provided an alternative perspective on the nature of the Thirty Years War. He re-emphasised the long-term roots of the conflict and distinguished not so much between causes internal and external to the Empire as between old and new types of expansionism. Western Europe saw a conflict between traditional powers, like Spain, and the 'new hegemons seeking expansion', especially France and the Netherlands. The same applied in central and northern Europe, where the traditional authority of the Emperor and the Habsburgs was challenged by the expansionism of individual German states and Sweden. Gutmann argued that 'the hegemonic explanation of the causes of war demands an old power or an old system reacting to the threat of a new power'. All the ingredients of the Thirty Years War existed during the second half of the sixteenth century. These might have been removed during the first two decades of the seventeenth century but were actually exacerbated by weak leadership which allowed long-standing rivalries to break through the surface. The end result was 'a new power formula in Europe, one in which the Habsburgs played a much smaller role'.

a firm religious grounding at the Jesuit University of Ingolstadt and established a fund, known as the 'aerarium', specifically for the defence of Catholicism. Frederick, like his predecessors, promoted a militant brand of Calvinism and made the Palatinate the defender of the Protestant faith in Germany. The two rulers were for some years leaders of rival confessional groupings: Maximilian of the Catholic League and Frederick of the Evangelical Union.

There were, however, major differences between them. Maximilian of Bavaria balanced his religious zeal with other qualities. For example, he quickly proved adept at managing Bavaria's finances, creating a surplus in the process. Frederick managed only to bankrupt his dominions and provoked widespread opposition to his rule in Bohemia; according to Steinberg, 'Frederick's kingship was based only on the radical wing of the selfish nobility who used him as their tool for maintaining their own power'. He was also unsuccessful in his quest for foreign allies. The Dutch offered only subsidies; his father-in-law, James I of England, drew back from being dragged into a major continental war; and Denmark intervened only after he had been deposed and his capital, Heidelberg, captured. Maximilian, on the other hand, was one of the most astute diplomats of the entire period. He made himself indispensable to the Emperor, whose reputation he did much to salvage during the 1620s, while at the same time negotiating with France to try to counterbalance what he saw as the excessive power of the Habsburgs. Although Maximilian failed to prevent the frequent invasion – and devastation – of Bavaria, he was one of the War's survivors. Frederick, by contrast, was one of its first victims.

Military commanders

The Emperors and state rulers rarely led their armies or even appeared on the battlefield. For this they relied upon professional soldiers. The first of these to advance the Imperial and Catholic cause was Count Tilly, a Bavarian general appointed by Duke Maximilian. A contemporary was the Count of Pappenheim, a Lutheran convert to Catholicism who served the Catholic League from 1620 and was appointed a general in the Spanish cavalry in Lombardy in 1625 before entering the Imperial service in 1626. Another was the Count of Gallas, who had extensive experience with the Spanish and Bavarian armies before being made commander-in-chief of the Imperial armies after 1634. Confronting the Imperialists were those, like Ernst von Mansfeld, Hans George von Arnim, and Bernard, Duke of Saxe-Weimar, who fought on the Protestant side.

They were, however, overshadowed by their contemporary from Bohemia, Count Wallenstein. By judicious purchase of estates confiscated from the Bohemian rebels of 1618, Wallenstein became one of the wealthiest landowners in the Empire. Contracted by Ferdinand II to provide and lead an Imperial army, Wallenstein demonstrated his considerable military skills by defeating Mansfeld at Dessau Bridge (1626), before proceeding to overrun Mecklenburg, Holstein, Schleswig and Denmark. On reaching the Baltic he had conferred upon him the honorary title of General of the Oceanic and Baltic Seas. The year 1629, however, proved a turning point in his career. When he failed to capture Stralsund and showed reluctance in enforcing the Edict of Restitution, there were loud murmurings against him at the Imperial court. Succumbing to pressure, the Emperor dismissed Wallenstein in 1630, although he had to recall him the following year after the disastrous Imperialist defeat at Breitenfeld. Wallenstein proved less successful during his second term as commander-in-chief, losing the Battle of Lützen in 1632. When he subsequently tried to negotiate a peace settlement with Saxony, Brandenburg and Sweden, he was accused of treason. The Emperor dismissed him a second time, declared him an outlaw and placed a price on his head. Wallenstein's career came to an abrupt end with his assassination in 1634.

Wallenstein was the most baffling and contradictory personality of the entire period. For example, his capacity for self-discipline and hard work in pursuit of his ambitious policies was counterbalanced by periods of inactivity and lethargy. He was also intensely superstitious – despite being a convert to Catholicism – and consulted astrologers regularly throughout his career. The complexity of his character makes him more difficult to categorise than any of his contemporaries; he seems to have been part-mercenary, part-diplomat, and part-political aspirant. It has been agreed, on the one hand, that he was a selfish and corrupt opportunist produced by an age of chaos and degeneration. Alternatively, he has been seen as an outstanding figure among a host of mediocrities, combining military genius with a deep understanding of political reality.

Wallenstein could certainly be seen as an above-average commander, more effective than Tilly if less radical than Gustavus Adolphus. At the same time, his political awareness was far more extensive than that shown, for example, by von Arnim or Bernard of Saxe-Weimar. The source of his frustration was that he possessed a real understanding of the key issues of the day but lacked the means of doing anything about them; he was unwilling, or unable, to take the ultimate step of converting his military leadership into political power.

The earlier part of his career certainly seems the more constructive. This was the period of his most striking military success which destroyed the first major threat from a foreign interventionist power and brought the Habsburg presence to the Baltic. He also displayed unrivalled energy in Bohemia – in the organisation of his estates, in the pursuit of a coherent economic policy and in an unusually extensive provision of education. Above all, he swam against the current of religious fanaticism. He was profoundly unhappy about the ideological emphasis of the Edict of Restitution and was convinced that Imperial success could not result from forcible reconversion. But he failed to persuade the Emperor to pursue a pragmatic course and his reluctance to implement the changes demanded by the Edict contributed to his first dismissal.

The period between his recall and his assassination has come to be dominated by the historical debate on the motives behind his nefarious diplomatic activities. His negotiations behind the Emperor's back have been variously ascribed to a burning desire for revenge for his dismissal in 1631; to a genuine desire to bring peace to a region devastated by foreign intervention; and to ambitions for personal territorial gain and political ascendancy. Wallenstein has been seen both as a traitor to the Habsburgs who employed him, and as a potential liberator who might, given the resources he needed, have liberated Bohemia and united Germany. The issue is as controversial as ever, although more emphasis is now placed on Wallenstein being overwhelmed by the pressure of events. Maland, for example, argues that Wallenstein lacked a coherent strategy, finding himself increasingly in 'a situation of tortuous complexity'.

The Swedes

Gustavus Adolphus

No-one had a more direct influence on a particular phase of the Thirty Years War than Gustavus Adolphus. Most aspects of his career have been dealt with elsewhere in this pamphlet, but it would be useful to draw together the main threads.

His first contribution was to provide Sweden with a domestic base strong enough to enable her to participate on equal terms with European powers with greater resources and larger populations. On his accession in 1611, Sweden was not even the mistress of the Baltic: that position still belonged to Denmark. But a series of domestic reforms made a substantial difference. He achieved a harmonious and productive relationship with the *Riksdag* (legislature) and *Riksrad* (Council); he laid the foundations for the collegiate system which was to make Sweden's administration the most efficient in Europe; he extensively overhauled local government and education; and he stimulated rapid industrial expansion, partly by establishing connections with Dutch entrepreneurs like Louis De Geer, and partly by gearing industries closely to the requirements of warfare. Above all, he achieved internal harmony – between the various social classes and between Church and State.

As a statesman his main impact on Europe was undoubtedly between 1630 and 1632. There has been some debate about his personal beliefs and his motives for becoming involved. The traditional view, reflected in 1890 by C. R. L. Fletcher, is that he was primarily 'the champion of Protestantism'. N. Ahnlund connects this with political ambitions: Gustavus Adolphus 'strove to bring the interests of Sweden into harmony with the general interests of Protestantism'. M. Roberts goes a stage further: Gustavus was essentially empirical, dealing with situations 'as they arose, by successful expedients'. It makes most sense, however, to see him as a statesman whose intentions expanded to fill the space created by his victories. His motives were initially the defence of his realm against the Habsburg threat and the preservation of Protestantism. He subsequently became more and more ambitious – especially with regard to Germany. The very success of his earlier pragmatism enabled him to think in the broader ideological terms which clearly influenced his *Norma Futurarum Actionum*.

Whatever his motives, he succeeded, during the very brief period of his involvement, in changing the course of the War and reversing a previously unstoppable Habsburg tide. As explained in Chapter 5, he made a major contribution to the military changes of the seventeenth century. The Swedish armies which sliced through Germany in 1631 were based on a modified form of conscription, used advanced weapons, and were drawn up in a new and revolutionary formation. It is true that Gustavus Adolphus has been too generously credited with military innovation, but this does not diminish the shockwaves sent through Europe by the Battle of Breitenfeld in 1632. His commitment to Sweden's war effort was total; but he lacked the sense of perspective which would have prevented him from hurling himself into the heart of the battle and dying in a ditch at Lützen in 1632.

Oxenstierna

Fortunately for Sweden, this was not a failing of Axel Oxenstierna, Chancellor between 1612 and 1654. A lifelong friend of Gustavus Adolphus, Oxenstierna is often seen as the instrument by which the dead king's policies continued to be implemented. He had a wealth of administrative and diplomatic experience which enabled him to carry Sweden through the regency of Queen Christina. His first priority was to protect Sweden's political stability. Hence, in 1634, he incorporated in the Form of Government all the administrative changes he had previously helped Gustavus Adolphus to design. He also ensured careful financial management and the development of Sweden's extensive copper resources.

The continuity was less obvious in the conduct of the War. Although he accepted that complete withdrawal was out of the question as long as any residue of the Habsburg threat remained, Oxenstierna did not entirely share the enthusiasm of Gustavus Adolphus for the War and twice redefined the scope of Swedish participation.

In the first place he attached a limited objective to Sweden's relations with the Protestant German States. For example, he regarded the League of Heilbronn not as the practical means of achieving the political objectives outlined in Gustavus Adolphus's *Norma Futurarum Actionum*, but as a way of reducing the size of the Swedish armies and placing upon the German states more of the responsibility for their own defence. Even this brought strong opposition from those within the council in Stockholm who were conscious of the strain on Sweden's resources; at times, indeed, Oxenstierna himself became thoroughly disillusioned, complaining that 'we pour out blood here for the sake of reputation, and have nought but gratitude to expect'.

Oxenstierna adjusted his course a second time when the League of Heilbronn was smashed at Nördlingen in 1634 and some of the Protestant states, led by Saxony, made their peace with the Emperor. What was left for Sweden? According to Roberts, 'Though institutional security might now be unattainable, territorial security, as it had first been conceived in 1630, was still a necessity.' Oxenstierna's perseverance brought eventual territorial compensation, particularly the coastline of Pomerania which he had never doubted Sweden should possess, together with the substantial indemnity of 5 million Reichsthaler.

Does all this mean that Oxenstierna completely lost – or never had – the ideological motivation which had helped drive Gustavus Adolphus in the earlier phase of the War?

Clearly his perception of Swedish interests pointed away from any idea of a crusade on behalf of Protestantism. On the other hand, he could hardly abandon the Protestant cause altogether. Improvement in Sweden's military situation in the 1640s, with the victories of Torstensson, meant that Swedish diplomats were able to press for concessions in the peace negotiations, such as the confirmation of Lutheran rights and inclusion of Calvinism for the first time. Yet one cannot help feeling that what mattered most to Oxenstierna – and to the Emperor – was territorial gain. Anything else was supplementary, if not incidental.

The French

Richelieu

The two Cardinals who controlled French foreign policy between 1624 and 1661 provided another example of continuity. Richelieu, who dominated the scene until his death in 1642, believed essentially in the power of diplomacy and intrigue. In his *Political Testament* he emphasised the need 'to negotiate everywhere without cease, openly and secretly'. This approach dominated the earlier period of his administration. He fostered close relations with the maritime powers, drawing up the Treaty of Compiègne with the Dutch in 1624 and arranging a marriage between Henrietta Maria and Charles I of England in 1625. He also promoted discord between the German states and the Emperor at the Diet of Ratisbon in 1630, and made effective use of Sweden as a military surrogate after 1631. It seemed that he had discovered the ideal method of dealing with the Habsburg threat: using others to probe the weaknesses of Austria and Spain while committing military resources only to peripheral areas, like the Valtelline in northern Italy.

Richelieu was, however, sufficiently a realist to see that this could not last indefinitely. 'In politics', he conceded, 'one is guided more by necessities than by predetermined wishes.' From 1635 onwards he was no longer able to guide events but was, instead, driven by them. He entered the War earlier than he had intended, largely because of the threat of Sweden's withdrawal, with the unfortunate initial results covered in Chapters 1 and 2. At this stage, however, he also displayed powers of resilience, and led the French recovery which culminated in the victory over the Spaniards at Rocroi which he did not live to see.

Mazarin

Cardinal Mazarin was the ideal successor. Trained by Richelieu, he was well versed in his methods. Their aims were broadly similar, and the usual interpretation is that Mazarin harvested the crop sown by Richelieu. What Richelieu initiated, Mazarin consolidated, pursuing with single-minded determination the humiliation of Spain and Austria and greatly strengthening the French frontier. In the process, however, he experienced the frustration of the protracted diplomacy which preceded the settlement at Westphalia. He made one major error of judgement in the process. Although he had hoped for a rounded settlement which would include both Austria and Spain, he broke his agreement with the Dutch that he would not negotiate separately with Madrid. He found himself pre-empted by the Treaty of Münster which deprived him of an ally and left him with an enemy. He nevertheless achieved an eventual triumph in his foreign policy, gaining by the Treaty of the Pyrenees (1659) even more than he had originally expected in 1648. The cost, however, was two major rebellions in France and near financial collapse.

4

Religious issues in the War

The principal religious changes between 1555 and 1648

This section will explain the main religious changes in the light of the key documents of the period: the Religious Peace of Augsburg (1555), the Edict of Restitution (1629), the Peace of Prague (1635) and the Peace of Westphalia (1648). The overall trend was the gradual disintegration of the religious settlement of 1555 and an erratic movement towards a new compromise in 1648. The years 1555–1618 saw attempts by both radical Protestantism and revived Catholicism to dominate the Augsburg Settlement. At first, Catholicism seemed to triumph and the Edict of Restitution wiped out all the gains made by Protestantism since 1552. The fortunes of the latter, however, revived in the 1630s through the intervention of Sweden. The Peace of Prague represented partial recovery and a move away from the Edict of Restitution. Further compromise followed in the Peace of Westphalia after another period of bitter conflict.

Rights of rulers

By Articles 15 and 16 of the Religious Peace of Augsburg, 'freedom of religious belief, liturgy and ceremonies' was to be allowed for both the 'Augsburg Confession' (Lutheranism) and the 'Old

Religion' (Roman Catholicism). But the freedom to adopt one of these faiths was given to authorities – the princes, Electors and estates – who had the *ius reformandi* (right to reform), and not to their subjects. During the period which followed Augsburg the position was summarised by the phrase, 'cuius regio, eius religio' (the ruler decides the religion). There were, however, two restrictions. The authorities were to avoid putting pressure on neighbouring estates to change their beliefs and, by Article 24, they were to place no obstacles in the way of any subjects wishing for religious reasons to emigrate.

These conditions proved surprisingly durable and were altered neither by the Edict of Restitution nor by the Peace of Prague, both of which focused more directly on ecclesiastical lands. The Peace of Westphalia confirmed the principle of 'cuius regio eius religio', although the ruler's *ius reformandi* was increasingly to be interpreted not so much as his right to interfere in the religious faith of his subjects as his 'authority to regulate the manifestations of religion in the life of the community' (H. Holborn).

One of the weaknesses of the Peace of Augsburg was that the religious divisions which it had recognised were not enshrined within the institutions of the Holy Roman Empire. For this reason the Empire's constitution folded up when placed under the strain of the Donauwörth Crisis of 1608. The Peace of Westphalia corrected this deficiency by ensuring that religious diversity was guaranteed by the Empire's constitution. In future, no religious changes could be made by simple majority vote within the Diet. Instead, approval was required from two new chambers established to try to provide a religious balance: the *Corpus Catholicorum* and the *Corpus Evangelicorum*. Similarly, the *Reichskammergericht*, or Imperial Cameral Tribunal, was to have a balance of Catholic and Protestant judges.

Ecclesiastical lands

There was somewhat less continuity in this area and the situation following the Augsburg settlement was highly complex. There were two types of ecclesiastical land. One, comprising Church property within secular states, was covered by Articles 18 and 19 of the Peace of Augsburg. These stated that all such property secularised by the time of the Treaty of Passau (1552) might remain

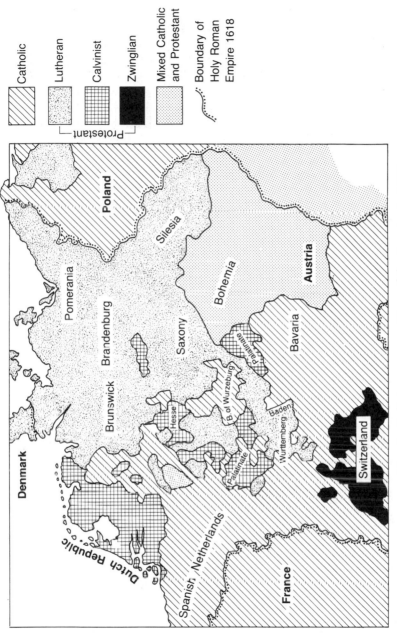

Map 3 Religious composition of the Empire in 1618

Catholic

Lutheran

Calvinist

Zwinglian

Mixed Catholic
and Protestant

Boundary of
Holy Roman
Empire 1618

Protestant

Denmark

Dutch Republic

Poland

Pomerania

Brandenburg

Brunswick

Silesia

Saxony

Hesse

B. of Wurzeburg

Palatinate

Bohemia

Baden

Wurtemberg

Palatinate

Bavaria

Austria

Spanish Netherlands

France

Switzerland

under its new owners, but that any Catholic abbot or bishop converting to Lutheranism after this date would automatically forfeit his lands and revenues to a properly elected Catholic successor. The second type was the much larger Imperial ecclesiastical estate, the ruler of which would be a prince bishop or archbishop; indeed, three such rulers, the Archbishops of Trier, Mainz and Cologne, were among the six Imperial Electors. Although such estates were not covered directly by the Treaty itself, they were soon brought within the scope of the Augsburg settlement by Imperial edict, much against the wishes of the Lutheran states. Under this order, known as the Ecclesiastical Reservation, these estates were to remain permanently under Catholic rule.

After 1555 there were several attempts to bring ecclesiastical estates under Protestant control. One of these failed: in 1583, the Archbishop Elector of Cologne was overthrown after he had tried to impose a Protestant Reformation within his Archbishopric, and a more reliable successor, Ernest of Bavaria, was installed. But two other estates, the Archbishoprics of Bremen and Magdeburg, did change hands, in defiance of the Ecclesiastical Reservation.

Church property within secular states was more widely affected. Where possible, Lutheran rulers ignored the restriction placed on secularisation after 1552 and the cumulative displeasure of the Emperors expressed itself in 1629 in the Edict of Restitution. This announced that Imperial commissioners would be sent into the Empire to 'reclaim all the archbishoprics, bishoprics, prelacies, monasteries, hospitals and endowments' possessed by the Church in 1552, and to install 'duly qualified persons' in them. Failure to comply with the Edict of Restitution would incur an automatic Imperial ban and possible military action by Tilly. Although secular rulers did what they could to circumvent the Edict, a considerable amount of property was reclaimed for the Church.

The partial recovery of the Protestant states in the early 1630s was reflected in the Peace of Prague. By Article 4, Church lands were to be returned to, or remain with, those who had actually owned them in 1627. The Peace of Westphalia then took the 'normal year' back to 1624. Although the Protestant states had wanted the dividing line to be 1618, the outcome did have the effect of returning many of the lands confiscated by the Edict of Restitution.

Calvinists

One of the major shortcomings of the Peace of Augsburg was the exclusion, by Article 17, of Calvinism and other sects. This seemed to have little effect on the spread of the 'Geneva Confession' which drew strength from its doctrine of predestination and the flexible organisation set out in Calvin's *Institutes of the Christian Religion*. Despite its rapid spread between 1555 and 1618, Calvinism received recognition neither from the Edict of Restitution nor from the Peace of Prague. The former specifically stated that 'all other doctrines and sects, whatever names they may have, not included in the Peace [of Augsburg] are forbidden and cannot be tolerated'.

It was therefore left to the Peace of Westphalia to clear up the anomaly and to end the myth that Calvinism did not exist. According to Article 7:

> It is agreed by the unanimous consent of His Imperial Majesty and all the Estates of the Empire that whatever rights and benefits are conferred upon the states and subjects attached to the Catholic and Augsburg faiths . . . shall also apply to those who are called reformed [Calvinists].

There was, however, a limit: 'Beyond the religions mentioned above, none shall be received or tolerated in the Holy Empire.'

Rights of subjects

Individual subjects benefited from the Peace of Augsburg only if they practised the same religion as their ruler. There was no universal toleration for minorities, although princes were, as we have seen, requested to allow dissidents to emigrate. Neither the Edict of Restitution nor the Peace of Prague made any further changes. The Peace of Westphalia, however, made important concessions to the private practice of religious belief. All subjects had conferred upon them the right to enjoy such freedom in the practice of religion as they had possessed in 1624, whether this freedom had been based on law or custom. In other words, subjects could now follow their beliefs in private; the power of the ruler was confined to regulating public religious policy. In those states where

35

individual freedom of religious observance had *not* existed in 1624, rulers were encouraged to show toleration. They did, however, have the formal right to expel dissidents for a period of up to five years, although the latter could hold property while in exile. The subjects of the Habsburg lands were less fortunate, since the Peace of Westphalia allowed the Emperor to withhold from them toleration of any kind. In theory, at least, the Austrian dominions remained the most intolerant in central Europe.

In practice, few rulers insisted in the future on any remaining right to impose uniformity on their subjects. In most states in central and western Europe the passion went out of religious observance, with the result that there was a comparative lull in ideological conflict for 150 years after 1648. The one major exception was France. Among the most pragmatic of states in the first half of the seventeenth century, she reverted, under Louis XIV, to a course of bigotry, with the withdrawal of Huguenot rights in 1685. Yet, significantly, this evoked a wave of opposition among Catholic and Protestant states alike and there was never any possibility of the sort of religious alignment which had existed during the Thirty Years War.

Was the Thirty Years War a 'war of religion'?

There has been a long-standing historical debate as to whether the Thirty Years War was the last – and greatest – of the wars of religion.

The traditional view was expressed by A. Gindely in 1884: 'The cause of the murderous war which, for thirty years of the seventeenth century lacerated Europe, is to be sought chiefly in the incompatibility of religious views which prevailed among the peoples of the time.' This line of argument is still pursued; G. Pagès, for example, stated in 1949 that the War 'witnessed the last effort of the Roman Church and the House of Habsburg to re-establish by a victory of Catholicism over Protestant heresies and the renewal of the universal role of the Emperor'. Such views are not, however, held by those who attach greater importance to political or economic considerations; according to F. Mehring, 'religion was as little the final cause of such developments as any ideology' (trans. by T. K. Rabb).

There is, of course, some evidence of religious influences on the origins of the War and within its various phases, although it is important to recognise other factors at work as well. Despite Mehring's assertion, ideology did play a major role. All the major leaders, with the single exception of Wallenstein, were heavily influenced by their religious beliefs. All the Electors of the Palatinate from Frederick III onwards were staunch Calvinists who allowed their foreign policy, before and after 1618, to be dominated by their obsessive belief that there was a Catholic conspiracy to destroy Protestantism. For its part, the Catholic Church experienced a period of revival and missionary zeal. Pope Gregory XV, for example, set up the Congregation for the Propagation of the Faith which organised the reconversion of those parts of the Empire conquered by the Catholic League and the Imperial armies in the 1620s. The Emperor Ferdinand II was undoubtedly driven by religious zeal (see p. 00) and was heavily influenced by the Jesuits at his court in Vienna. He frequently consulted his confessor, Lamormaini, and the influence of the Jesuits can be seen in the Edict of Restitution (1629), the dismissal of Wallenstein, and the hard line from 1630 onwards against the German Protestant states. Maximilian of Bavaria had an even more consistent record of defending Catholicism (see p. 00). Non-German statesmen also professed quite openly the influence of their faith. Gustavus Adolphus, a committed Lutheran, insisted on holding prayers on the battlefield, while even the supposedly pragmatic Richelieu stated that he 'abhorred heresy' and that he looked forward to a time when it could be eradicated in France.

On the other hand, there are too many inconsistencies to push very far the argument that this was even predominantly a religious war. Dynastic and pragmatic motives were of crucial importance and should not be dismissed, as they are by C. J. Friedrich, as merely reinforcing 'the basic religious urge'. For example, the policies of some of the leading German states were far from consistent, suggesting either political opportunism or an attempt to avoid being dragged into ideological disputes. Two examples are especially striking.

Lutheran Saxony supported the Emperor against Bohemia in 1619, joined Sweden against the Emperor in 1631 and threw in its lot for a second time with the Emperor in 1635. Each of these decisions was influenced more by political than by religious considerations. The Bohemian Revolt of 1618 threatened the fabric of the Empire, which the Elector of Saxony considered it important to preserve –

a view which was no doubt strengthened by the Emperor's offer of part of Lusatia in return for Saxony's support. By 1631 Saxony herself was under direct threat from the Habsburgs and Catholic League, and hastened to join Sweden, whose motives she had previously mistrusted, after Tilly's sack of Magdeburg. After 1635 it was once more in Saxony's interests to assist the Imperial cause, although in an intermittent manner which prevented her from being devastated by Sweden.

In Catholic Bavaria, Maximilian's religious considerations were heavily influenced by pragmatism. It is, of course, true that he contributed much to the early successes against the Bohemian rebels and against Protestant German states like the Palatinate, Baden and Brunswick. But he always stopped short of committing Bavaria fully to the Austro-Spanish bloc, even though this offered the only real prospect of rolling back Protestantism in Germany. Indeed, he sought a check to the power of Austria and Spain by conducting his own negotiations with France, even though Richelieu was committed to Protestant Sweden. In 1631, therefore, Bavaria joined France in a defensive alliance, a clear indication that Maximilian was deeply concerned about the possibility of territorial expansion by Spain and Austria in the area of the Palatinate where, of course, he had his own plans.

The great powers, too, were extensively influenced by strategic or dynastic motives. Sweden feared, above all, Habsburg expansion to the Baltic, and Gustavus Adolphus's plans for Germany were, above all, political. After the death of the Swedish King in 1632, Oxenstierna tried to implement his proposals and it is significant that the document establishing the league of Heilbronn in 1633 contained only one clause addressing religious issues. French policy was, of course, consistently opportunist throughout the War. The primary concern of both Richelieu and Mazarin was to contain the Habsburg threat in its twin manifestation of Spain and Austria. The protection of Catholicism was quite incidental to this; on occasions French policy had of necessity to risk damaging Catholic interests within the Empire. Even the Papacy pursued a line which was sometimes not in the interest of the Counter Reformation. For example, the main fear of Urban VIII (1623–44) was that the Emperor would try to extend his influence in Italy. He therefore ended Papal subsidies to Ferdinand II after 1623 and refused to provide assistance against the Swedish threat in 1631. He was even secretly delighted at the success of Gustavus Adolphus against the Habsburgs in 1632.

It seems, therefore, that there were as many examples of conflicts *within* religious groupings as there were *between* them. Yet it might be argued that most of the protagonists sought most of the time to integrate political and religious interests. Political objectives might be given a religious rationale. Gustavus Adolphus, for example, was able to combine Sweden's strategic struggle against the Habsburgs with a defensive war against 'Papism', while Spain and Austria justified their action against rebellion in the Netherlands and Bohemia as a crusade against heretics. But in those instances where political and religious interests diverged for any length of time, 'reason of state' always took precedence over ideology.

5

Military developments in the War

Importance of the period for warfare

It would be a reasonable assumption that one of the longest, most extensive and most destructive conflicts in modern history should have made a major contribution to the theory and practice of warfare. Yet the extent of this influence is the subject of a controversy between historians such as M. Roberts, who consider that the seventeenth century saw a 'revolution in warfare', and those, like G. Parker, who prefer to consider the War as an important part of a longer period of change.

Roberts identifies four ways in which warfare was transformed in the first half of the seventeenth century. First, he argues that it was profoundly influenced by tactical changes introduced in the Dutch Republic by Maurice of Orange and by subsequent adaptations made during the Thirty Years War by Gustavus Adolphus. Second, these had a major impact on the strategies employed in campaigns and battles. The new developments inevitably meant, third, that the scale of warfare became more extensive. Finally, this, in turn, had a major impact on the economy, society, rulers and subjects of the various states of Europe. Parker accepts the importance of these developments but, at the same time, questions the emphasis previously given to the roles of Maurice of Orange and Gustavus Adolphus.

This chapter will summarise the innovations made in warfare during the period, but also explore the idea that there was a degree of continuity. The latter can be understood in two ways. On the one hand, there were certain progressive influences from the sixteenth century. On the other hand, there were also habits and trends which considerably slowed the pace of change.

Tactics, strategy and weapons

The tactical manoeuvres of armies in the sixteenth century had been limited by the traditional pattern of battle formations. The main force in any army was the pikemen, who were drawn up in three or four large rectangles, known as squadrons or battalions, which were twice as deep in formation as they were broad. Smaller units of musketeers were attached to the corners of the squadrons or were deployed in the spaces between. The cavalry's main function was to move up towards the enemy ranks and fire their pistols from horseback before retiring to reload. In the meantime, another wave would discharge its salvo, the whole process being known as the 'caracole'. The main disadvantage of such tactics was that movement on the battlefield was unwieldy and ponderous. Of the pikemen, in particular, only the first few ranks could take a direct part in the battle. The others made up the bulk of the squadron and, in effect, remained immobile until those unfortunate enough to be in the front ranks had been thinned out.

During the late sixteenth century several major changes were introduced, mainly by the 'Dutch School' comprising Maurice of Orange, William Louis and Count John II of Nassau. In order to make more effective use of his manpower, Maurice of Orange reduced the size of infantry and cavalry units and entirely altered their shape. The infantry were now drawn up in ranks ten deep and the cavalry five deep. The rectangular formations were replaced by more extended lines, the pikemen in the centre flanked by the musketeers, cavalry and artillery. The overall result was greater flexibility in the use of both cavalry and infantry. More effective and sustained firepower was achieved by use of successive ranks which alternated between firing and reloading their muskets. Such developments fully proved their worth at the Battle of Nieuwpoort in 1600, when the Dutch inflicted a severe defeat on a Spanish army.

41

The Dutch reforms were further adapted during the Thirty Years War by Gustavus Adolphus who, in the process, gave the Swedish armies a major advantage over their opponents. The infantry was involved more extensively in the battle with the reduction of the number of ranks from the standard ten used in the Dutch army to six and even, on occasions, to three. This was made possible by the introduction of two formidable weapons. One was a shorter pike which could be used as effectively in attack as in defence. The other was a lighter musket which could be loaded and fired much more quickly since it did not require the support of the traditional forked rest. The cavalry, meanwhile, became a more formidable proposition. No longer advancing, discharging firearms and then withdrawing, it was ordered to charge the enemy with drawn sabres. The headlong charge, an unnerving – even terrifying – experience for the enemy, was complemented by another change introduced by Gustavus Adolphus. This was a more flexible use of artillery. Traditionally, heavy guns had been confined to discharging cannon balls from predetermined points on the battlefield, usually with minimal effect. Gustavus Adolphus introduced lighter artillery pieces which could be moved during the course of the battle and concentrated on the enemy's most vulnerable points. The Swedes possessed overwhelming superiority in cannon from the time that Gustavus Adolphus included eighty 3-pounders in his invasion force in 1630. His tactics consisted of a concentration of musketry and artillery firepower against the opposing infantry. Once holes had been torn in the enemy lines, these would be systematically opened up by cavalry charges and by the advance of the infantry units with their redesigned pikes. The results were the defeats inflicted on the Imperial forces by Gustavus Adolphus at Breitenfeld and Lützen and by his successors at Wittstock and Jankow. Encouraged by the success of such methods, the Swedish commanders went out of their way to seek decisive engagements and they managed to conduct several campaigns within the same season.

Despite the evidence for major changes in the conduct of warfare during the first half of the seventeenth century, use of the term 'military revolution' is open to criticism on the grounds that there were precedents in the sixteenth century or earlier. The Italian Wars, for example, are now increasingly seen as a time of experimentation. It would also be a mistake to assume that the Spanish armies, which are thought to epitomise the traditional style, had not undergone at least some change before the Thirty Years War. The Duke of Alva had introduced musketeers into virtually every unit during the 1550s, while experiments had taken place in the cavalry with both lancers and gunmen; although the caracole dominated their tactics, the concept of the full-blown charge was not entirely unfamiliar to Spanish commanders. Similarly, the importance of artillery may have been boosted by Gustavus Adolphus, but most sixteenth-century commanders had made extensive use of heavy guns on the battlefield.

It could also be argued that many of the changes of the Dutch and Swedish Schools were incompletely applied during the Thirty Years War, or that they were often unsuccessful when they were applied. The linear formations of Gustavus Adolphus certainly worked during his campaigns between 1630 and 1632. After his death, however, the size of the Swedish armies shrank steadily, which meant that the original flexibility of the linear formations had to give way to considerations of economy. Other Protestant states applying the principles of Maurice of Orange were unable to survive militarily against the Habsburgs and Catholic League; Frederick of the Palatinate and Bohemia, Christian of Denmark and Christian of Brunswick were all defeated by traditional methods employed by Spinola, Tilly and Wallenstein respectively. Indeed, Parker points out that it was not the Protestant states employing new techniques who came closest to ending the war. 'The two battles of the war which came nearest to achieving "total" victory were, as it happened, won by Spanish "old-style" forces: White Mountain in 1620 and Nördlingen in 1634.'

The size, composition and supply of armies

One of the major developments of the period of the Thirty Years War was the enormous growth in the size of the armies of the competing powers. Spain, for example, mobilised 300,000 men during the 1630s, double the number she had kept in the field in the mid-sixteenth century. The Dutch Republic maintained 80,000 in the 1630s, compared with 20,000 in the 1590s, while the figures for Sweden during the same years were 120,000 and 15,000 respectively and, for France, 150,000 and 80,000. Even the Imperial forces topped 100,000, largely because of the private enterprise policies of Wallenstein. But the strains of the War eventually told and all governments had to reduce the size of their armies during the 1640s. Torstensson and Wrangel, for example, had to make do with Swedish armies of 15,000, while, in 1647, Imperial troops numbered only 9,000 and Bavaria mustered 10,000. These numbers were much more in keeping with those of the sixteenth century, although the long-term trend was steadily upwards; by the end of the seventeenth century, for example, Louis XIV was able to put 400,000 French troops into his campaigns.

How were the armies of the Thirty Years War recruited? One of the features of the military 'revolution' of the early seventeenth century was the growth of national armies based, at least partly, on conscription. The administrative basis was provided in Sweden by an Ordinance in 1620 and by the overlapping of recruiting areas with local government jurisdiction; the evolution of the province-based regiment was to be widely imitated, particularly in England. At the same time, there was a certain element of continuity with the sixteenth century, which had first seen the emergence of the prototype of national standing armies. Conversely, the Thirty Years War saw numerous examples of the survival of more traditional recruiting arrangements. Wallenstein's agreements with the Emperor in 1625 and 1632 were an indication of the latter's inability to follow the general trend towards national forces. Even those governments which were able to make the adjustment still had to rely heavily on the oldest of all military expedients – the employment of mercenaries. These were particularly in evidence in the Dutch and Swedish armies; it has been estimated, for example, that only 20 per cent of the troops serving under Gustavus Adolphus at Breitenfeld were Swedes, and fewer than 18 per cent of those at Lützen. The main recruiting grounds for the Protestant states were France, England and Scotland, while the Spanish monarchy relied heavily on Irishmen and Poles. The motives for signing on as a mercenary varied widely, ranging from the search for employment and escape from rural poverty to the prospect of excitement and plunder.

In some respects the organisation and drill of armies in the seventeenth century were greatly improved. Count John II of Nassau produced an illustrated manual for the use of weapons by the infantry, breaking the whole process down into numbered stages which facilitated co-ordinated action. Standards of discipline were also more carefully defined, particularly by Gustavus Adolphus in the Swedish Articles of Law in 1621. The success of such measures was, however, mixed. The Thirty Years War had more than its share of mutinies, usually over delays in payment, and all commanders experienced extreme difficulty in maintaining discipline when their troops capured any centre of population, whether a small town or a city like Magdeburg, which was sacked in 1631. It could, of course, be argued that the commanders themselves set a bad example by assuming that any offensive should end automatically in plunder. Even Gustavus Adolphus regularly transferred huge quantities of German valuables to Stockholm and Uppsala, while General Königsmarck, who led the Swedish assault on Prague in 1648, authorised the capture of booty worth 7 million thaler.

All the governments participating in the War found the financial strain enormous. The problem was not, of course, without precedent, since, between 1585 and 1604, both the Dutch Republic and Spain had borrowed heavily and entered the new phase of conflict already in debt. To some extent, rulers met the situation by raising extra taxes; any representative institutions which tried to call a halt were battered into submission. There were, however, limits to this, as Philip IV discovered when his increased demands for contributions to the Spanish war effort drove Portugal and Catalonia into revolt in 1640, to be followed in 1647 by Naples. It has been argued that royal absolutism developed in the seventeenth century as a direct response to the need to centralise control over the military resources of the state. If this is indeed the case, it became most apparent, especially in Brandenburg and France, in the decades *after* the Thirty Years War. Before 1648 this aspect of the 'military revolution' was certainly incomplete.

6
The impact of the War on society and the German economy

Sources

Contemporary sources have been drawn on extensively by historians to document civilian suffering during the War. Among the most influential have been two major works published during the course of the seventeenth century. One of these was Pufendorf's *The Conditions of the German Empire*. Pufendorf was a professor of international law and served in both Sweden and Brandenburg as official historiographer. His work provided considerable detail about the conditions in Germany during and immediately after the War. But perhaps the best known of contemporary writers was Grimmelshausen, author of *Simplicius Simplicissimus*. This work provided harrowing details of the torture and killing of peasants and their families by Swedish and mercenary soldiers and of the revenge taken by the peasants against army stragglers. The War also produced a host of diaries providing vivid first-hand descriptions; these are given special poignancy when compared with the illustrations produced during the period. Three types are shown here: a heavily stylised painting by Wouwermans; detailed engravings by Callot and Meyer; and the somewhat cruder etchings of Franck.

How reliable are illustrations likely to be as sources? It is rare for them to convey accurately an actual event. In some instances the artist may well be creating an entirely fictional scene, using contemporary warfare merely as a theme. The painting by Wouwermans tells us as much about the artistic conventions of the mid-seventeenth century as about the type of engagement fought. The etchings by Franck are, in contrast, intended to convey a message about the suffering inflicted on each other by marauding mercenaries and peasants. They show, in the process, no concessions to artistic style. The works of Callot and Meyer are perhaps a combination of the two, attempting to use a sophisticated art form to make a statement about the miseries of war. Callot was especially influential and several accounts in Grimmelshausen's *Simplicius Simplicissimus* seem to have been based closely on Callot's illustrations.

The most difficult task for the historian of the Thirty Years War is to achieve a balance between individual and personal accounts on the one hand and, on the other, the sweeping generalisations of contemporary writers and artists. Several types of source are of use here. One is statistical material, which can be extracted in a variety of forms. For example, district chroniclers like Heberle described in precise detail the sale of horses and supplies to the Swedes during the occupation of Ulm in 1646. Alternative sources are tax records, of which an extensive collection is available for Bohemia, or the details assembled by estate managers. Historians have also attached importance to records showing the payment of tolls in German ports like Hamburg.

Statistical data are often considered to be inherently one of the most reliable forms of primary source because they are likely to be the most neutral. On the other hand, they may well have been manipulated, either by contemporaries or by modern secondary sources seeking to support a particular thesis. This may involve careful selection, omission, even distortion. In any case, most statistics are meaningless until an historian makes clear his or her reason for referring to them. This will nearly always means editing, and therefore interpretation.

In addition to statistical information there are also various types of registers and records of estate proceedings. These provide detailed material on specific administrative problems in individual estates and are invaluable for any analysis involving a cross-section study. Again, however, they may have been subject to selective editing, either at the time or by more recent writers.

Historians are by no means agreed on the actual usefulness of primary sources in building up a composite picture of the effects of the War on the Empire. Very few now allow contemporary descriptions of misery to dominate an entire interpretation. Yet some, like C. J. Friedrich, acknowledge that there is a sufficient range of sources to provide a balanced assessment and to show that the effects of the War varied widely throughout the Empire; this could be taken as an endorsement of their value. By contrast, S. H. Steinberg is more critical of their worth, arguing that the sources most used – chronicles, annals, diaries, letters –

> chiefly show the events of the war as experienced by those who lost most. For the compilers of town chronicles, parish registers, family albums and personal diaries all belonged to the same class of educated, professional men – clerks, priests, officials, lawyers – who were hit hardest by the vicissitudes of the times.

Debate on the effects of the War

Steinberg's approach to the social and economic impact of the War is doubly revisionist. Not only does he question whether it was accurately described by those who lived through it; he also refutes the long-standing assumption that the War was a disaster for Germany's civilian population.

This view had been due in large measure to Gustav Freytag (1816–95), who had made extensive use of the type of source described above to show that a once great 'German nation' had been utterly devastated by the conflict. Steinberg traces the pedigree of the 'disastrous war school' back to Pufendorf, who, he argues, had deliberately magnified the extent of the destruction at the instigation of Frederick William, the Great Elector. The latter felt the need to justify some of the tough policies which he adopted after 1648 against the peasantry, the estates and the townspeople and, in Steinberg's words, 'the dark picture which he painted of the war years was meant to highlight the magnitude of his political, economic and cultural successes'.

The 'disastrous war school' has, nevertheless, been remarkably persistent and a significant number of twentieth-century historians would agree with the view of D. Ogg in 1925 that 'in no other instance of modern warfare did the civilian population suffer so much as in this'. The main challenge has come from two directions.

1 Philips Wouwermans: *Cavalry Making a Sortie from a Fort on a Hill* (National Gallery, London)

2 Etching by Franck of violence committed on villagers by marauding soldiers (Germanisches Nationalmuseum, Nuremberg)

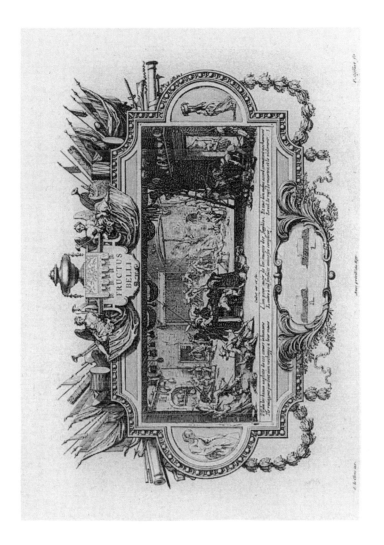

3 Jacqués Callot: *Les Misères de la Guerre* (Ashmolean Museum, Oxford)

4 Engraving by Rudolf Meyer showing a peasant appealing to an officer (Staatliche Graphische Sammlung, Munich)

The first is the case made by Steinberg that the evils of the War were exaggerated and that Germany suffered far less than is commonly supposed. This, however, is less widely accepted than the argument that the War caught the Empire during a period of weakness and accelerated a trend which was already apparent. In the words of A. J. P. Taylor: 'It was not the cause of German decline and weakness, but rather the result. The impoverishment, the dwindling of the cities, the decay of cultural and material standards, all these had been proceeding for a century before the Thirty Years' War broke out.'

The rest of this chapter will consider the impact of the War in the light of Steinberg's arguments and of the 'disastrous war' and 'earlier decline' schools.

Impact on the population

The basic criterion for the impact of the War on German society is the loss of population. This can be gauged partly by military, partly by civilian casualties.

The Thirty Years War saw an unusually high proportion of deaths in battle and during extended campaigns. At Breitenfeld, for example, 8,000 of the 31,000 Imperial troops were killed; Swedish losses at Nördlingen amounted to 50 per cent; and over 60 per cent of the Saxon and Imperial troops died at Wittstock. The proportion of casualties was so high largely because of the introduction of new battle tactics, especially by Gustavus Adolphus; as we have seen, these included devastating cavalry charges and more intensive and accurate use of artillery.

Figures like this tell us that soldiering was a far more hazardous occupation than it had been in the sixteenth century, when the chances of being killed in any particular battle had been quite small. They do not, however, contribute much to the overall picture of population loss, which particularly affected non-combatants. Civilians were in direct contact with armies of both sides, which not only lived off the land but also indulged in pillage and destruction on a massive scale. Commanders were unable to impose military discipline of the type which would be taken for granted in the wars of the eighteenth century. Even worse was the need to repeat campaigns as military leaders failed to accomplish their objectives at the outset. Some areas were therefore subject to

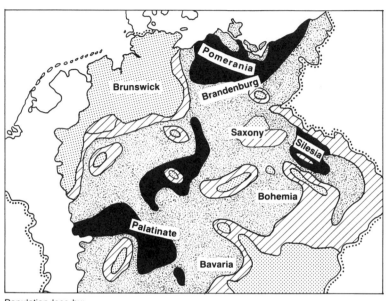

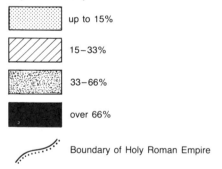
Map 4   Destruction in the War

54

incessant disruption, as well as to the famine and disease brought by the armies.

It would appear logical to assume a heavy loss of population from the countless repetition of such incidents. Some figures indicate an overall decline in the population of the Holy Roman Empire from 21 million in 1618 to 13.5 million by 1648. During the same period the population of Bohemia has been said to have fallen from 3 million to 800,000, with 29,000 of her 35,000 villages being deserted during the conflict. Urban centres are also considered by some historians to have suffered severely; Augsburg, the largest German city, with 48,000 people in 1620, had only 21,000 in 1650. Magdeburg lost 25,000 of her 30,000 inhabitants in the notorious sack of 1631. The areas worst affected were the Palatinate, with losses of up to 80 per cent, Bohemia, Pomerania, and parts of the Rhineland, Brandenburg, Silesia and Bavaria.

Steinberg's challenge to this traditional picture is based on the view that primary sources exaggerated the extent of Germany's population losses for a variety of motives, including the understandable desire of urban authorities to keep to a minimum their financial contributions to the war effort. Steinberg concedes that some areas did experience heavy losses: in certain districts of Thuringia, for example, these reached 66 per cent. On the other hand, such losses were not permanent since they were due to migration rather than death. The rapid growth of population in Thuringia immediately after the end of the War indicated that the evacuees had returned. The picture was the same throughout the war-affected areas, while the cities which saw little or no fighting actually increased in size. Overall, Steinberg maintains, Germany suffered no demographic catastrophe. If anything, the Empire's total population probably grew during the War from between 15 and 17 million in 1600 to between 16 and 18 million in 1650.

The current tendency is to reduce the earlier figures for population loss without going as far as Steinberg in asserting that there was no net loss at all. A reasonable estimate would be an overall decline of between 15 and 20 per cent, from a total of 20 million to between 16 and 17 million. It is also possible to show that the Empire had made a complete demographic recovery by 1700 rather than continuing, as was once believed, with a smaller base until the nineteenth century. In all probability the German population trend was, for the seventeenth century as a whole, broadly in keeping with that of other European countries, none of which showed much of an increase between 1600 and 1700. The main difference was that Germany suffered her losses during the period of the Thirty Years War, while France's losses occurred in the wars and famines of the second half of the century. Thus, although the War was considered devastating to those who experienced it at first hand, it was by no means unique in Europe's extensive experience of destructive conflict.

Impact on cities and rural areas

It was once thought that the Thirty Years War brought about the collapse of a thriving German economy. The proponents of the 'disastrous war' school have, however, been outnumbered by those historians who consider that the Empire was already in economic decline before 1618 and that, although the War may have accelerated the process, it did not begin it.

There is considerable evidence for this. Most of the cities of the Empire had already been adversely affected by political and commercial developments during the sixteenth century. The reign of Charles V (1519–56) had seen the misuse of Germany's resources in pursuit of an over-ambitious foreign policy which was bequeathed to his son, Philip II (1556–98). Spanish foreign policy after 1556 had depended heavily on loans from German bankers, particularly the Welsers and Fuggers, both of whom had been badly affected by the bankruptcies of Philip's reign. Meanwhile, the peripheral powers had been gaining increasing control of the main volume of trade. The cities of the Hanseatic League, so dominant in the Middle Ages, had been undermined by Sweden in the Baltic, while simultaneously three commercial powers had risen in the west: England, France and the Netherlands. More and more trade was therefore beginning to bypass the Empire.

If, however, economic decline was under way before the 1620s, there is a strong case for arguing that the process was accelerated during the Thirty Years War. For one thing, the Empire suffered severely from the great inflation of the early 1620s, the primary cause of which was the sudden shortage of precious metals from the New World and consequent devaluation. For another, the population decline inevitably affected urban economies, as did the enormous demands placed on the remaining inhabitants by military commanders in search of the means to finance their campaigns. When the War had run its course many cities failed to recover their earlier economic and political strength. The Imperial Free Cities especially became a prey to the surrounding German states, some of which – like Brandenburg – perpetuated the habit of financial exactions for military purposes.

The War also helped create a commercial vacuum in central Europe. The conditions of warfare between 1618 and 1648 rarely favoured the usual practice of conducting military campaigns and trade simultaneously, and in some areas the destruction was such that the normal trade links were severed. As a result the peripheral routes became more important. Germany was further affected by the Peace of Westphalia, which gave control over the outlets of major rivers to foreign powers. For example, the Netherlands controlled the mouths of the Rhine, and Sweden the outlets of the Weser, Elbe and Oder. Consequently, when trading contacts were renewed with Germany, they were conducted to the advantage of the foreign powers, who could now impose tolls on the routes under their control.

There were, of course, major exceptions. Hamburg, which was only lightly touched by the War, experienced a population growth and a considerable expansion in its trade, which enabled it to become the largest and most prosperous of all German cities. Danzig and Lübeck also benefited, although on a somewhat smaller scale. Elsewhere there were examples of recovery, such as Leipzig, which rose from ruin to become Germany's second trading city. But for every Hamburg and Leipzig there were several Augsburgs and Magdeburgs which never regained their previous importance and wealth.

German agriculture entered the seventeenth century in crisis. Like many other parts of Europe the Empire experienced a collapse in agricultural prices which produced a prolonged recession. The War, however, made things infinitely worse. The armies of both sides brought destruction and instability which prevented settled agriculture, while depopulation, whether permanent or temporary, severely reduced the labour force.

The long-term effects of the War varied from area to area. F. L. Carsten draws a distinction between southern and western Germany on the one hand and north-eastern Germany on the other. In the former, especially Bavaria and the Palatinate, the War accelerated the decline of serfdom, already under way before 1618. The decline of the peasant population reduced the number of tenants available and therefore increased their bargaining powers with the nobility.

In the north and east, however, the nobility were more powerful and the decline of the peasant population had the unfortunate effect of tightening serfdom. This applied especially in Brandenburg, where the landed nobility, or Junkers, appealed to the Great Elector to issue edicts to this effect; they used the reduced numbers of peasants as an excuse to continue with a longstanding policy of evictions and estate consolidation. In this they were fully supported by the Great Elector, who worked on the principle of increasing the social powers of the nobility in return for their unremitting political allegiance. In the longer term this was to become one of the key factors in the development of autocratic rule in Brandenburg-Prussia.

Impact on German culture

The traditional view is that the Thirty Years War had a profound effect on almost all aspects of German culture, creating a wilderness which lasted until the late eighteenth century. The period saw no great German artists and, according to Ogg, Germans were 'obliged to borrow from Shakespeare' because they 'failed to produce a national poet'; however, German appreciation was less for Shakespeare's 'vigour and originality' than for his 'coarseness and violence'. The writers of the eighteenth century blamed on religious fanaticism the brutality and philistinism which they held to characterise seventeenth-century Germany, while in the twentieth century Bertolt Brecht looked back to the era of the Thirty Years War to make statements in *Mother Courage and her Children* about militarism and cultural deprivation which were really an attack on Nazi Germany. The War, in other words, became synonymous with barbarism and cultural deprivation.

In challenging this picture, Steinberg advances the case that there was not only a remarkable continuity in cultural achievement, but that Germany actually 'reached new heights' in areas like lyrical poetry. The traditional view, he argues, was dominated by the 'aesthetic standards' of nineteenth-century critics, to whom the seventeenth-century German baroque style was 'anathema'. Now that the mid- and late twentieth century has restored baroque to its rightful historical place, it is possible to appreciate the importance of German poets like Dach, Gerhardt, von Spee, von Logau and Silesius. The novelist Grimmelshausen can be compared with Bunyan, the author of *A Pilgrim's Progress*, while the contributions of Kepler to astronomy are self-evident. It is also possible to point to a vast outpouring of journalistic endeavour in the form of news-sheets and newspapers. Finally, of course, late seventeenth-century Germany produced J. S. Bach, the foremost composer of his age.

In the light of this argument, the balance should perhaps be reset. On the other hand, it may be that here, as elsewhere, Steinberg has overstated his case. The notion of a complete cultural vacuum and a period of barbarism should be dispensed with, but not to the extent of arguing that there was no cultural decline at all. The point surely remains that in all areas of intellectual activity except music and astronomy, Germany was outclassed by other parts of Europe. It has to be said that the literary names cited by Steinberg are somewhat obscure when compared with French writers like Racine and Molière, or with Milton in England. Germany produced no great artist in the seventeenth century. Although the Thirty Years War provided the theme for numerous painters and engravers, the most impressive results were the work of the French Callot or the Dutch Wouwermans.

It might be said that, well into the eighteenth century, German cultural development followed two courses. One was a continuous evolution of a native culture which had been weakened, without actually being destroyed, by the depredations of the Thirty Years War. The other was the massive influence of the French Enlightenment in Germany, especially in the Prussia of Frederick the Great. Then, in the second half of the eighteenth century, the German strain reasserted itself in the form of the German Enlightenment represented by Kant and Goethe. By comparison with *their* achievements, the output of German literature and philosophy in the hundred years after 1648 had been lean indeed.

7

The Peace of Westphalia

It is rare for a peace settlement to be drawn up swiftly. But the negotiations to end the Thirty Years War were, by any standard, interminably prolonged.

The first attempt was made as early as 1634 by Pope Urban VIII who tried to bring together France, Spain and the Emperor. Although delegates assembled at Cologne in 1636, the whole enterprise fell apart because of the absence of Protestant representation. The Emperor Ferdinand II took over the initiative in the same year when he convened a meeting of the Electors at Ratisbon. His successor, Ferdinand III, sought to establish contacts with Denmark, Sweden, England, France and Spain; in 1640 he summoned the full Diet to Ratisbon, which held over 150 sessions during the course of the next eighteen months. All these attempts proved abortive and it was not until 1644 that negotiations were held in earnest in the Westphalian towns of Münster and Osnabrück. Even then the proceedings were dragged out for over four years before the Treaties of Münster and Osnabrück – known collectively as the Peace of Westphalia – were finalised.

The first reason for this delay was the unusually complex and intricate diplomatic procedures adopted by the participants. Twenty-five miles separated the two conference centres – and the Protestant and Catholic delegations. The Swedes and German Protestants were based at Osnabrück, while the French, Spanish and Imperial representatives, along with the German Catholics, used the facilities at Münster. The first six months were dominated by diplomatic protocol, questions of precedence and even the order of processions. As well as the obvious differences between the two sides, there were also conflicts between allies. Sweden and France were notoriously uncooperative, while the Archbishop Elector of Trier frequently opposed the Emperor's interests. There were even differences between delegates of the same country: between, for example, Servien and d'Avaux of France, and the Swedes, Salvius and Oxenstierna. To make matters even more complicated, the German representatives were divided, at both centres, into the three traditional chambers of the Imperial Diet – Electors, princes and cities. Negotiations were pursued in parallel and agreement was necessary at each level as well as between levels. The whole process was subject to constant interruption, delay or complication. The representatives of the major powers, for example, received instructions from their governments which were frequently changed.

Second, the whole peacemaking process was complicated by the range of issues involved. These were religious, territorial, constitutional, affecting both the Empire and the powers. Motives constantly shifted. At times some of the parties involved would be trying to accelerate the move towards agreement, while others would be seeking to strengthen their position in anticipation of renewed conflict; within weeks the roles might be reversed. Much depended on the degree of success or failure on the battlefield, on the prospect of a new alliance, or on the severity of economic pressures at home. The Emperor, for example, was unusually obstructive in 1644 because he knew that Sweden was preoccupied by a war with Denmark, while military success in Germany encouraged France and Sweden to increase the pressure after 1646. The War was ended only when the interests of all the powers converged in 1648: Austria faced catastrophic defeat, Spain and the Netherlands made an unexpected bilateral peace, Sweden was exhausted economically, and France was confronted by political crisis.

How did the Peace of Westphalia affect its participants?

The religious terms of the Treaties of Osnabrück and Münster have been dealt with in detail in Chapter 4. This section therefore concentrates on political and territorial changes affecting the Empire and the major European powers.

The Empire and the German states.

Considering the length and the savagery of the Thirty Years War, there was no dramatic transformation in the political structure of the Holy Roman Empire. The number of territorial units remained unaltered at about 350, while the Imperial Diet still comprised the traditional three chambers, with the additional voting procedure on religious issues involving the *Corpus Catholicorum* and the *Corpus Evangelicorum*.

On the other hand, the settlement did acknowledge openly a long-term trend which the struggle had accelerated, namely the decentralisation of Imperial authority and the growing autonomy of the individual states. For example, Articles 64 and 65 of the Treaty of Münster conferred upon the princes of the Empire the power of *Landeshoheit*. This enabled them to draw up on their own initiative treaties with powers outside the Empire, provided that these were not actually directed against the Emperor. The Emperor, in turn, now had to acknowledge the failure of the centuries-old attempt to bring the territorial princes back into line. Furthermore, he now had to secure the consent of these princes before making any treaty on behalf of the Empire, raising troops or imposing taxation. Between 1648 and its eventual dissolution by Napoleon in 1806, the Empire never again functioned as a political unit. The future belonged, instead, to a select number of individual states.

These were affected in different ways by the Peace of Westphalia. Of the handful who had defied the Emperor in the 1620s, Brunswick emerged in 1648 strengthened by the acquisition of the conference centre of Osnabrück. The Palatinate, on the other hand, was severely punished for the Elector Frederick's decision in 1618 to accept the Bohemian crown: the Peace of Westphalia confirmed all the gains already made at the expense of that unhappy state. This left the Lower Palatinate, which was returned to Frederick's son, Charles Louis. This area had, however, been devastated during the War and was never again to achieve pre-eminence within the Empire.

Of all the German states, Bavaria had shown the most consistent support for the Habsburg and Catholic cause: apart from a brief period between 1647 and 1648 she had been at war since 1618. Her reward was the Upper Palatinate and an Electorate, which guaranteed Bavaria's continuing importance within the Empire. On the other hand, she had suffered severely in expended resources and population loss. It might even be argued that, since Bavaria's gains had been made by 1629, the next two decades, which involved the greatest destruction, had achieved nothing. Certainly Bavaria had been frustrated in her religious mission of spreading the Counter Reformation within Germany, although she had, of course, played a vital role in underpinning the Catholic defences after 1630.

By comparison with Bavaria, Brandenburg achieved territorial additions disproportionate to her actual contribution to the course of the War. Her involvement had been confined to the period 1631–41, in support initially of Sweden and then of the Emperor. The Elector Frederick William had used his troops to gain and occupy new territory, which ensured that he was in a stronger diplomatic position than his fellow princes. In addition he secured permanent Dutch support by marrying into the House of Orange, and managed to convince Mazarin that a strengthened Brandenburg would do much to forestall any future Swedish designs in northern Germany. Admittedly, the Elector's initial attempt to gain the whole of Pomerania foundered on strong Swedish counter-claims, so that Brandenburg had to content herself with eastern Pomerania only. However, there was handsome compensation for losing western Pomerania to Sweden; Brandenburg received the Archbishopric of Magdeburg and the Bishoprics of Halberstadt and Minden. She also had confirmation of her sovereignty over the Duchies of Cleves and Ravensberg, originally ceded to her in 1614 by the Treaty of Xanten.

The Peace of Westphalia made possible the eventual emergence within the Empire of another great German power in addition to Austria. The Elector Frederick William carefully consolidated Brandenburg's gains, at the same time building up Hohenzollern absolutism by securing the unconditional obedience of the nobility in return for conferring on them increased powers over the peasantry. Within the space of thirty years Brandenburg was challenging Sweden's position in northern Germany; in just over a century Prussia was to become the most efficient military power in Europe, able under Frederick the Great to hold her own against a combination of Austria, France and Russia.

There are two ways of looking at Austria's position in 1648.

On the one hand, Austria had suffered severe defeat during the last phase of the War, particularly at the Battle of Zusmarshausen. She had experienced extensive devastation as a result of the all too frequent campaigns of Swedish armies on Habsburg territory. And, with the settlement in Germany, the Habsburgs now had to abandon much of their Imperial authority over the princes. To make matters even worse, the close connection with the Spanish Habsburgs was finally severed. Spain and Austria now had no common objectives to pursue in their foreign policies and any residual commitment to a crusade to enforce the Counter Reformation on central Europe had long since disappeared. For the first time in nearly 150 years, therefore, Austria lacked a 'natural' ally in Europe. Her decline should, by this analysis, have been a logical consequence of both the War and the Peace.

This does not, however, provide a fully accurate picture. In several respects Austria's position in 1648 was less serious than might be supposed, owing largely to the negotiating skill of her chief plenipotentiary at Westphalia, Trautmannsdorf. He managed to avoid converting Austrian military losses in the last phase of the War into territorial losses at the conference table by conceding to the victors territory which was part of the Empire but not directly under Habsburg rule. The only exceptions to this were southern Alsace, ceded to France, and Lusatia, which had already been sold to Saxony in the early 1620s as part of a deal to ensure the latter's support against the Palatinate and the rebels of Bohemia.

In some respects Austria actually benefited from the settlement. Whatever Ferdinand III lost in terms of Imperial powers he more than gained as head of the Habsburg dominions; indeed, his authority over the latter was much more certain than had been that of Rudolf II or Mathias before 1618. Vienna was now the capital of a more centralised state, the various provinces of which were brought firmly into line for the first time. Despite its various disadvantages, the War ended the separatist ambitions of Bohemia, Moravia and Silesia, which now became hereditary possessions of the Habsburgs. Similarly, Westphalia left it open to Austria to pursue its own religious policy and did not replicate the permanent division between Protestant and Catholic which was part of the settlement in Germany. The Austrian Habsburgs may not have achieved their designs in relation to the Empire, but they cannot have been displeased at what had been accomplished in their own lands. After 1648 Austria became a major power in her own right and, unable to expand within the Empire, sought outlets elsewhere. The most immediate aim now was the recapture of the Hungarian plains from the Turks, a mission which had been achieved by the end of the seventeenth century. In 1713 Austria also extended her territory both in Germany and Italy, as a result of the surrender of extensive Spanish possessions by the Treaty of Utrecht.

Sweden

Swedish gains from the Treaty of Osnabrück were substantial. In addition to being paid a war indemnity of 5 million Reichstäler, Sweden received western Pomerania, Stettin, Wollin, Wismar, Rügen and the Bishoprics of Bremen and Verden. These possessions also guaranteed her representation in the Imperial Diet, something which had been denied to her ally, France. She controlled the outlets of the Elbe, Oder and Weser, as a result dominating the flow of trade in the Lower Saxon and Westphalian Circles. She also appeared to have achieved the main objectives of Gustavus Adolphus in 1630: throwing back the Habsburg advance to the Baltic, gaining a Swedish presence within Germany and guaranteeing the survival of Protestantism within the Empire.

Yet there was a residual feeling of dissatisfaction. Sweden's military success during the 1640s had led her plenipotentiaries, Salvius and Oxenstierna, to advance substantial demands. They had bid for an indemnity of 12 million Reichstäler, together with the whole of Pomerania and, to provide a base in the heart of Germany, the Habsburg province of Silesia. They had also claimed one of the electoral college votes, which would have given Sweden a voice in future elections of the Emperor. Ultimately, however, Sweden had had to settle for less than her military success seemed to have deserved. There were two reasons for this. First, France had followed whatever course was necessary to limit Swedish claims, which meant that if Sweden had wished to accomplish all her aims she would have had to achieve total victory by herself. Second, however, Queen Christina had quickly grasped that this was beyond Sweden's capacity; convinced that Salvius and Oxenstierna were delaying proceedings unnecessarily, she had put pressure on them to achieve the possible rather than the preferable.

The territory ceded at Westphalia proved in the long run to be a mixed blessing. At first Sweden was able, by the Treaty of Oliva (1660), to consolidate her hold on the north German coastline. Certainly there could now be no doubt that she had become the major power in the Baltic, and her support continued to be sought for the rest of the century, particularly by Louis XIV. At the same time, these extra possessions proved a major liability to a country which had a small population and very limited financial resources. They also brought her into direct conflict with Brandenburg by whom she was defeated at the Battle of Fehrbellin in 1675; this sapped her strength for the more extensive Great Northern War. By 1721, Bremen, Verden and most of western Pomerania had been divided between Brandenburg-Prussia and Hanover, while to the east of the Empire, the Swedish presence on the Baltic shores had been ended by Peter the Great's Russia.

France

French gains from the Treaty of Münster were numerous but, as Map 5 shows, geographically disconnected. Possession of Metz, Toul and Verdun, which had originally been acquired before 1559, was now confirmed. France also received part of Lorraine, together with Breisach in southern Alsace. In addition, she was granted a Landgravate over, but not outright possession of, the rest of Alsace and 'provincial prefectures' over ten Imperial cities within the area. The largest piece of territory was the Sundgau, the furthest removed was Pinerolo in northern Italy.

Taken as a whole these acquisitions were less extensive than those of either Sweden or Brandenburg. There is no doubt that Mazarin had hoped for more. In December 1647, for example, he had instructed Turenne 'to consider Alsace a country which belongs to the King no less than Champagne does'. The situation within France, however, forced him to end the war in Germany as quickly as possible so that he could concentrate on the real enemy – Spain. He had already increased loans to unprecedented levels, sold public offices, raised existing taxes and levied new ones, and delayed the payment of interest on public debts and *rentes*. Even his sudden willingness to compromise at Westphalia failed to prevent

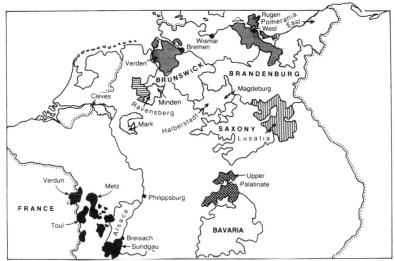

Territorial gains:

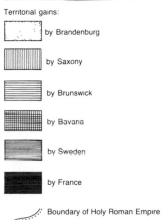

    by Brandenburg

    by Saxony

    by Brunswick

    by Bavaria

    by Sweden

    by France

    Boundary of Holy Roman Empire

Map 5   Peace of Westphalia

a rapid increase in his own unpopularity and the outbreak of two major rebellions, or Frondes.

It is, however, arguable that 1648 marked an important milestone in the longer-term military ascendancy of France. The limited gains, made mainly at the expense of Austria, were to be used to extract far more substantial territorial acquisitions in the continuing conflict with Spain. French penetration into Alsace imposed a stranglehold on the military routes to the Spanish Netherlands and made it possible for France to outflank Spanish Franche Comté from the north. During the course of the next half-century Louis XIV sliced off large areas of Spanish territory along the French frontier, adding parts of the Spanish Netherlands by the Treaties of the Pyrenees (1659) and Aix-la-Chapelle (1668), and Franche Comté by the Treaty of Nijmegen (1678). During the 1670s and 1680s Louis XIV also used the gains made in 1648 to increase French involvement in the affairs of the Empire, aiming at one stage at the Imperial crown itself. Although this particular quest was to prove unsuccessful, there can be little doubt that the period from 1648 onwards saw the completion of most of Richelieu's original ambitions: the separation of the Spanish and Austrian Habsburgs, the expansion of the French frontier into the Empire, and the substitution of French for Spanish military supremacy in Europe.

Spain and the Netherlands

Although there had been a Spanish delegation at Münster, news of Spain's separate treaty with the Dutch Republic in 1648 jeopardised any chance of her participation in a general settlement. The Peace of Westphalia did not, therefore, deal with the conflict between France and Spain in Franche Comté and the southern Netherlands. The war between the two countries continued for a further eleven years until it was eventually concluded by the Treaty of the Pyrenees (1659) by which Spain lost substantial territory. Nevertheless, the Peace of Westphalia had a direct impact on Spain. French territorial gains along the Rhine imperilled the Spanish presence in Flanders and Franche Comté and enabled the greater resources of France to be brought fully to bear on a power which was exhausted by eighty years of continuous conflict and deprived of the support of Austria. By 1648, Spain's position as a major power was tenuous; by 1659 she was definitely in decline, a process accelerated over the rest of the seventeenth century by a series of costly and destructive wars with France.

For Spain, therefore, 1648 meant little more than the decision to pull out of one conflict in an ultimately fruitless attempt to salvage something from another. For the Dutch Republic, by contrast, the Treaty of Münster was the prize for nearly a century of struggle. The northern Netherlands were recognised as fully independent from Spain and were permitted to retain any conquests which had been made overseas, mainly at the expense of Portugal. The Dutch Republic was not even required to guarantee religious toleration to its residual Catholic population, although in practice repression would not have been in the interests of internal stability.

Yet, despite its obvious benefits, the Treaty of Münster did not end the cycle of warfare in which the Dutch had become caught up. Almost as soon as enmity with Spain had ceased, new rivalries developed. Largely for commercial reasons, the Dutch fought in quick succession three wars with England (1652–4, 1665–7 and 1672–4). More dangerously, they also became entangled in continental conflicts (1672–8, 1688–97 and 1702–13) with their previous ally, France. During the second half of the seventeenth century there was therefore no further increase in Dutch influence to act as a counterpart to the decline of Spain.

Was the Peace of Westphalia a turning point in European history?

Some peace conferences have aimed consciously at drawing up a settlement which would be both permanent and definitive. The delegates who devised the 1919 Versailles Settlement, for example, considered it their mission to ensure that the struggle between 1914 and 1918 should have been 'the war to end wars'. It is unlikely that the plenipotentiaries at Osnabrück and Münster had quite the same ambition. In part, their objective was to end one struggle in order to define and consolidate the position of their states for the next. It is, therefore, ironical that the settlement of Westphalia should have proved far more resilient and long-lasting than that of Versailles.

The extent of its influence on future developments in European history has, however, been subject to different views. On the one hand, G. Pagès considers that the period represents 'the transition from medieval to modern times in Western and Central Europe' and that Westphalia confirmed this, being 'the first truly European settlement in history'. C. V. Wedgwood, on the other hand, believes that the Treaty was, like most others, 'a rearrangement of the European map ready for the next war' and that it would be wrong to see it as an identifiable point of transition from one epoch to another.

There is much to support Wedgwood's argument. Those powers which increased their territories anticipated further gains in the future; Mazarin, as a pupil of Richelieu, certainly intended to push France's frontiers deep into Germany. The unsuccessful participants in the War, such as Spain and Austria, naturally aimed at recouping their losses as quickly as possible. It was, therefore, inevitable that Westphalia should be seen as a breathing space. At the same time, it had a significance which far transcended this. Indeed, it can be seen as one of the definitive treaties of modern history. Most settlements between 1648 and 1789 were to be modifications of Westphalia. For example, the Treaty of Utrecht (1713) reallocated many of Spain's possessions to Austria, and the Treaties of Aix-la-Chapelle and Hubertusburg (1748 and 1763) confirmed Prussian territorial gains at the expense of Austria. None of these, however, made any significant alteration to the boundaries or constitution of the Empire. The next settlement of more general significance to Europe as a whole was to be the Treaty of Vienna (1815).

The year 1648 has been seen as a turning point in a broader sense. A. Toynbee (*A Study of History*), and others have argued that the Peace of Westphalia brought to an end a period of religious fanaticism, introducing an era free from the tyranny of ideology for the next 150 years – until, that is, the next wave of fanaticism, under the label of nationalism, was released by the French Revolution. Although Westphalia did not end European wars, it did have a profound effect on the way in which warfare was conducted; according to Toynbee 'the immediate effect was to reduce the evil of war to a minimum never approached in any chapter of our Western history before or since'. The reason was that, between the ages of 'religious fanaticism' and 'nationalist fanaticism', warfare became more 'a sport of kings' and destruction was correspondingly reduced. W. Durant goes further still. He sees in the end of the Thirty Years War the transition to a more rational order which eventually produced, in the Enlightenment, an intellectual revolution as important as the Renaissance. 'The Peace

of Westphalia', he argues, 'ended the reign of theology over the European mind, and left the road obstructed but passable for the tentatives of reason.'

Toynbee and Durant cover within their perspective the broad sweep of civilisation. It is to be expected, therefore, that they deal in generalisations and that their view of any one period will lack the cut and thrust of alternative views; they do not, for example, consider the evidence for pragmatic and non-religious policies pursued before 1648. But this does not invalidate the general proposition that after 1648 there was a shift away from alliances based on ideologies towards those constructed for dynastic reasons. As a result the enemy became less hated and there was more incentive to avoid wanton destruction. In this sense the Peace of Westphalia, while not reducing the future incidence of warfare, did at least establish more civilised guidelines for its conduct.

Select bibliography

Selections of primary sources

G. Benecke (ed.), *Germany in the Thirty Years War* (London, 1978).
P. Limm, *The Thirty Years War* (London, 1984).
M. Roberts (ed.), *Sweden as a Great Power 1611–1697*. Documents (London, 1968).

Secondary sources

The New Cambridge Modern History, vol. IV: *The Decline of Spain and the Thirty Years War 1609–48/59* (Cambridge, 1970).
G. Parker, *Europe in Crisis 1598–1648* (Brighton, 1980).
D. Ogg, *Europe in the 17th Century* (London, 1925).
D. Maland, *Europe at War 1600–1650* (London, 1980).
C. J. Friedrich, *The Age of the Baroque 1610–1660* (New York, 1952).
W. Durant, *The Story of Civilization: The Age of Reason Begins* (New York and Geneva, 1961).
H. Holborn, *History of Modern Germany*, vol. 1 (New York, 1959).
A. J. P. Taylor, *The Course of German History* (London, 1945).
G. Parker, *The Thirty Years War* (London, 1984).
J. Elliott, *Imperial Spain 1469–1719* (London, 1970).
G. Pagès, *The Thirty Years War 1618–1648* (London, 1971).
C. V. Wedgwood, *The Thirty Years War* (London, 1938).

J. V. Polisensky, *The Thirty Years War* (London, 1970).

T. K. Rabb (ed.), *The Thirty Years War* (Boston, Mass., 1972).

A. Gindely, *History of the Thirty Years' War*, trans. A. Ten Brook (New York, 1884).

S. H. Steinberg, *The Thirty Years War and the Conflict for European Hegemony* (London, 1971).

H. Langer, *The Thirty Years War* (Poole, Dorset, 1980).

C. R. L. Fletcher, *Gustavus Adolphus* (London, 1890).

N. Ahnlund, *Gustav Adolf the Great*, trans. M. Robert (Westport, Conn., 1983).

M. Roberts, *Gustavus Adolphus: A History of Sweden 1611–32*, vol. II (London, 1958).

M. Roberts, *Gustavus Adolphus and the Rise of Sweden* (London, 1973).

G. Mann, *Wallenstein* (London, 1976).

J. H. Elliott, *Richelieu and Olivares* (Cambridge, 1984).

P. Brightwell, 'Spanish Origins of the Thirty Years' War', *European Studies Review* (1979).

P. Brightwell, 'Spain and Bohemia: The Decision to Intervene, 1619', *European Studies Review* (1982).

P. Brightwell, 'Spain, Bohemia and Europe, 1619–21', *European Studies Review* (1982).

M. P. Gutmann, 'The Origins of the Thirty Years' War', *Journal of Interdisciplinary History*, XVIII: 4 (Spring 1988).

G. Parker, 'The Thirty Years' War', *History Today* (August 1982).